D0193107

At a Glance

2nd Edition

A Practical Guide to Children's Special Needs

Viv East and Linda Evans

continuum

B0013630   371.9
£14.99

Continuum International Publishing Group

The Tower Building
11 York Road
London
SE1 7NX

80 Maiden Lane
Suite 704
New York
NY 10038

www.continuumbooks.com

© Viv East and Linda Evans 2006

All rights reserved. No part of this publication may be reproduced or transmitted in any form or by any means, electronic or mechanical, including photocopying, recording, or any information storage or retrieval system, without prior permission in writing from the publishers.

First published in 2001 by Questions
Reprinted in 2004 by Questions
Reprinted in 2005 by Continuum
Second edition published in 2006 by Continuum

British Library Cataloguing-in-Publication Data
A catalogue record for this book is available from the British Library.

Library of Congress Cataloging-in-Publication Data
East, Viv.
   At a glance: a practical guide to children's special needs /
Viv East and Linda Evans. – 2nd ed.
      p. cm.
ISBN-13: 978-0-8264-9151-0 (pbk.)
ISBN-10: 0-8264-9151-0 (pbk.)
1. Children with disabilities—Education—Handbooks, Manuals, etc.
I. Evans, Linda, 1954– . II. Title.
LC4015. E176 2006
371.9—dc22

2006025115

ISBN 0-8264-9151-0 (paperback) ⊢

Typeset by Servis Filmsetting Ltd, Manchester, England
Printed and bound in Great Britain by Bath Press, Bath, England

Contents

Introduction

Why 'at a glance'?

We wrote the first edition of this book five years ago, to provide a quick reference point for busy teachers and assistants. It proved to be immensely popular and useful to a whole range of people, and we have been delighted with its success.

This new edition has been updated and extended to include references to the national strategy for dealing with children who have special educational needs. The legislation and national initiatives outlined are those that apply to England. For details on policy in other areas of the UK, readers can refer to the websites below:

● Learning and Teaching Scotland: www.ltscotland.org.uk
● Welsh Assembly Department for Training and Education: www.education.wales.gov.uk
● National Council for Special Education in Ireland: www.ncse.ie

This new edition also covers some additional 'conditions' and syndromes. There are now more pupils with SEN in mainstream classrooms than ever before, and all teachers have to be aware of a wide range of learning needs and medical conditions.

We can't all be experts, but we can make sure that we have a basic understanding of the difficulties pupils encounter in school, and that we are armed with some practical strategies to help them. The SENCO (special educational needs coordinator) is a valuable source of information and advice but it is the responsibility of each and every teacher to 'remove barriers to achievement' for children who have additional needs.

This book covers all of the most frequently encountered conditions, arranged alphabetically in sections to enable quick access to the appropriate page, where you will find:

● A brief introduction to the condition, including possible causes and prevalence
● An explanation of the main difficulties as they manifest themselves in the classroom
● A range of practical strategies to try
● A useful address and/or website for further information (a list of additional contacts is included at the back of the book)
● Where appropriate, an example of an Individual Education Plan (IEP) is provided

Communication difficulties overlap with many of the syndromes and conditions covered in the book and so we have included information about Augmented and Alternative Communication (AAC) in the 'Learning Needs' section.

Throughout the book, we stress that each pupil is unique and that the key to successful teaching is to respond to individual needs and preferences. Teachers and assistants must be prepared to try different approaches, review, and change where necessary.

Consultation with parents/carers, other professionals involved with a child, and the child himself/herself is essential if a consistent, holistic and successful approach is to be achieved.

P.S. A note about left-handed writers:

Several readers took us to task about including 'left-handed writers' in the first edition, arguing that this does not constitute a 'special educational need'. Strictly speaking, we agree. But experience has taught us that teachers don't always understand that being left-handed in a predominantly right-handed world can have its disadvantages. Without sympathetic handling, left-handed writers can experience difficulties, lose self-esteem and indeed, *develop* special needs – quite unnecessarily.

INDIVIDUAL EDUCATION PLAN

Name:

Year:

Stage:

Area of concern: ADHD

Strengths: Likes to see finished work.

Teacher/Support:

Start date:

Review date:

IEP no.:

Targets:

1. To remain in his seat for at least 10 minutes.
2. To complete a task sheet for each lesson.
3. To achieve five rewards per week.
4. To work co-operatively with one other pupil.

Strategies for use in class:

1. Always maintain eye contact.
2. Make sure the task sheet contains short, easily achievable goals that will ensure success. More can be added once it is working well. In addition check that x understands what to do and takes responsibility for getting stars when completed.
3. It is important that each lesson contains a variety of activities.
4. Use the 'time-out' room when necessary.
5. Encourage x to help with tasks between lesson times to cut down opportunities for problems with peers.
6. Use teacher attention to praise good, on task behaviour.

Role of Parent(s)/Carer(s):

1. Calm routines in the morning before school.
2. Consistent messages.
3. Weekly liaison with school.

Success criteria:

1. To succeed with target on a gradual basis, beginning with one lesson, then two and so on.
2. Stars will be given for each time a target is hit.
3. x will work with one other pupil in PE and for science.

Resources:

1. Guidelines for all staff provided.
2. Task sheet template on computer.
3. 'Time-out' room.
4. LSA for 10 hours per week.

Agreed by:

SENCO:

Parent(s)/Carer(s):

Pupil:

Date:

Attention Deficit Hyperactivity Disorder (ADHD)

Attention Deficit Hyperactivity Disorder (ADHD) is a term used to describe children who exhibit over-active behaviour and impulsivity and who have difficulty paying attention. It is estimated that 0.5 to 1 per cent of children in the UK are affected by ADHD, and about five times more boys than girls are diagnosed with this condition. Children of all levels of ability can have ADHD. Some professionals feel that the term is becoming over-used and extended to include any child who is naughty, but research points to a substantial number of children demonstrating a range of behaviours which constitute a diagnosis of ADHD. In some more severe cases, the child may be treated with medication such as methylphenidate (Ritalin), which can have very beneficial effects: but this remains a controversial issue.

The main characteristics

- Difficulty in following instructions and completing tasks
- Difficulty in 'sticking to' an activity
- Easily distracted and forgetful
- Often doesn't listen
- Fidgets, is restless, can't sit still
- Interferes with other children's work
- Can't stop talking, interrupts others
- Runs about when inappropriate
- Blurts out answers without waiting to be asked
- Difficulty in waiting or taking turns
- Acts impulsively without thinking about the consequences

Although most children will demonstrate some of these behaviours some of the time, those who have several of these problems consistently, at home and at school, are likely to have ADHD. These children often find it hard to learn; research from the USA suggests that 90 per cent of children with ADHD underachieve at school, and 20 per cent have reading difficulties.

How can we help?

If parents are given support while their children are young, they may be able to prevent problems later on. Some key principles are as follows.

- Make eye contact with the child when speaking to him or her. If you call out from another room the child will ignore you.
- Keep instructions simple – the one sentence rule.
- Give very specific praise, catch the child being good.
- Keep calm – if you get angry the child will mirror that emotion.
- Use a 'quiet time' technique to deal with temper tantrums.
- Practise ways of distracting the child.
- Provide clear routines.
- Give advance warning when something is about to happen, or finish.
- Give two choices, avoiding the option of saying no: 'Do you want to put your coat on now or when we get outside?'

Teachers and other school staff can help children with ADHD by careful consideration of how they organize the classroom and how they themselves behave.

- Arrange the room to minimize distractions.
- Use a variety of activities in every lesson, alternating physical and sitting-down tasks.
- Set short, achievable targets and give instant rewards when the child completes tasks.
- Present text in large, well-spaced format without a lot of clutter on the page.
- Keep classroom rules clear and simple – and rehearse them regularly.
- Use checklists to help him work through a task or homework activity.
- Encourage the child to verbalize what needs to be done – first to the teacher then silently to himself.
- Use teacher attention and praise to reward positive behaviour.
- Give the child special responsibilities so that others see him or her in a positive light and the child develops a positive self image.

ADD Information Services offers advice to parents, young people and professionals:
PO Box 340, Edgware, Middlesex HA8 9HL
Tel: 020 8906 9068
ADDNET UK
www.btinternet.com/~black.ice/addnet/

INDIVIDUAL EDUCATION PLAN

Name:	**Area of concern:** Asperger's Syndrome
Year: 10	**Strengths:** Rote learning
Stage:	**Teacher/Support:**
Start date:	
Review date:	
IEP no.: 8	

Targets:

1. To act as a helper in computer club.
2. To develop an understanding of metaphors – x will work on the meaning of 10 common metaphors.
3. To complete each day's tasks and worksheet.

Strategies for use in class:

1. Remember to address x by name.
2. Make sure tasks are written down as well as explained so that x is prepared for what he has to do. Please remember to initial his worksheet.
3. Use x's strengths for remembering facts to boost self-esteem.
4. Use straightforward language.
5. Respect x's need for space and allow him to sit at the end of a row/desk.
6. Make use of computers whenever possible.

Role of Parent(s)/Carer(s):

1. To help with homework.
2. Regular contact with SENCO.
3. To reinforce work on metaphors.

Success criteria:

1. To be seen helping younger pupils rather than sitting at the computer by himself on at least five separate occasions.
2. To be able to explain a given metaphor from the ones being studied.
3. To hand in his worksheet at the end of each day showing each task has been completed.

Resources:

1. Special pack in staff room for use/advice.
2. Daily worksheet – copy in staff room.
3. x has a buddy – this is . . .
4. Use of 'time-out' room if needed.
5. Work with SENCO and SSA on social skills, how to help in computer club, etc.

Agreed by:

SENCO:

Parent(s)/Carer(s):

Pupil:

Date:

Asperger's Syndrome

Regarded by some as a distinctive condition, Asperger's Syndrome is viewed by others as the higher-ability aspect of the autistic spectrum. Individuals with Asperger's Syndrome can have symptoms ranging from mild to severe but tend to have serious difficulties with communication and social skills. Children often speak in a monotonous or exaggerated tone and at great length about topics that interest them. They avoid eye contact and often have obsessive, repetitive routines and preoccupations.

Because of their high degree of functionality and their naivety, those with Asperger's Syndrome are often thought of as 'odd', and are frequently a target for bullying. The causes of Asperger's Syndrome are still under investigation but research suggests that it may not be the result of a single factor but a series of neuro-biological triggers that affect brain development. Numbers affected are thought to be in the region of between 10 to 36 in every 10,000, with more males than females affected.

The main characteristics:

- **Difficulties with social relationships.** They find it difficult to read the signals which most of us take for granted and find it hard to interact with others.
- **Difficulties with communication.** They may speak very fluently but not take much notice of the reaction of people listening to them; they may talk on and on regardless of the listener's interest or may appear insensitive to their feelings. Despite having good language skills, people with Asperger Syndrome may sound over-precise or over-literal – jokes can cause problems as can exaggerated language and metaphors: e.g., a person with Asperger Syndrome may be confused or frightened by a statement like 'she bit my head off'.
- **Difficulties with social imagination, imaginative play and flexible thinking.** While they often excel at learning facts and figures, people with Asperger Syndrome find it hard to think in abstract ways. This can cause problems for children in school where they may have difficulty with certain subjects, such as literature or religious studies.

The child may also be:

- socially awkward and clumsy in relations with other children and/or adults
- naive and gullible
- often unaware of others' feelings
- unable to carry on a 'give and take' conversation
- easily upset by changes in routines and transitions
- literal in speech and understanding
- overly sensitive to loud sounds, lights or odours
- fixated on one subject or object
- physically awkward in sports.

They may have:

- unusually accurate memory for details
- sleeping or eating problems
- trouble understanding things they have heard or read
- inappropriate body language or facial expression
- unusual speech patterns (repetitive and/or irrelevant remarks)
- stilted, formal manner of speaking
- unusually loud, high or monotonous voice
- tendency to rock, fidget or pace while concentrating.

How can we help?

- Talk to parents!
- Be flexible.
- Prepare them for any changes well in advance – have a contingency plan for emergencies. At school, they may get upset by sudden changes, such as an alteration to the timetable.
- Have high expectations.
- Use their ability to remember by rote to increase self-esteem.
- Always refer to the child by name – they do not necessarily realize that 'everyone' includes them.
- Be calm – never shout.
- Modify facial expressions and body language – ensure the child has time to respond.
- Be precise with instructions, e.g. 'We are going outside now' *not* 'Shall we go outside?'
- Use concrete apparatus.
- Use visual lists, e.g. a daily timetable.
- Present small, manageable tasks with visual prompts.
- Acknowledge the need for personal space, e.g. allow them to sit on the end of the row in assembly.
- Provide a place for time out when they need it.
- Keep to a structured classroom – use labels, and specific areas for specific tasks.
- Apply rules consistently.
- Develop a buddy system if possible.
- Use stories to teach communication/social interaction.
- Ensure everyone who comes into contact with the child knows how to react, e.g. lunchtime supervisors, supply staff.
- Make good use of computers – they are not demanding in emotional terms, as people often are.

National Autistic Society
393 City Road
London EC1V 1NG Tel: 020 7833 2299
www.nas.org.uk
www.aspennj.org

Augmentative and Alternative Communication (AAC)

'*Communication is a basic human right, a need and a critical part of learning.*'
www.scope.org/education/aac.shmtl

'Communication' refers to the giving and receiving of information through the use of spoken words, signs, gestures, symbols or writing. Although all pupils have the right to access the curriculum, communication difficulties can prevent them from doing so effectively.

Augmentative and Alternative Communication (AAC) describes methods of communication that can be used by anyone who finds communication difficult because they have little or no speech. It adds to (*augments*) or replaces (*is an alternative to*) spoken communication. AAC can aid understanding as well as being a means of expression. It builds confidence and self-esteem.

There are two main types of AAC: **unaided** or **aided**, and most AAC users combine the two.

Unaided AAC: This does not require additional equipment but relies on people understanding the ways in which spoken communication can be augmented, e.g. by gesturing and pointing, eye movements, body language, signing, vocalizations.

Aided AAC: This requires additional equipment: anything from simple pictures to a highly technological voiced computer.

Aided AAC divides into two areas: low technology and high technology.

- **Low technology** aids include any additional equipment that is not powered. For example, charts, communication books using pictures or stick-on words, symbols or photos, pen and paper, objects of reference.
- **High technology** aids refer to the more complex systems such as specialized programmable electronic aids and computers that speak and print. Some pupils use alternative devices to control their aided AAC system, such as a switch, light pointer or a device to control an on-screen printer.

Who is it for?

It is vital that when high technology aids are to be taken into consideration, a thorough assessment is carried out. Making a good assessment and providing the most suitable communication solution for an individual is a careful, painstaking process. It is important to trial aids for a suitable length of time and, realistically, it will take about six months from a referral to any initial provision. Although this may seem a long time it must be remembered that throughout this period further developmental work will be carried out by therapists, teachers, parents and others.

A high technology aid will not be appropriate for all children or for all situations. There will be a small number of pupils with severe communication difficulties for whom high technology aids are found to be unsuitable after a series of trials.

High technology aids vary in price but tend to be fairly expensive.

In 2002 the government introduced the Communication Aids Project (CAP). Its aim was to help pupils who had communication difficulties by providing technology to:

- help them access the curriculum and interact with others
- support their transition to post-school provision.

Funding was made available to:
- assess the pupil's needs
- provide appropriate hardware and/or software
- train teaching staff
- train the pupil and parents/carers
- monitor and review.

As a result of this many Authorities set up local multi-agency assessment teams and many more children and young people with severe communication needs had access to modern, high technology aids. The funding was time limited until 2006 but the legacy that has been left in many areas of the country is highly-skilled assessment teams and a policy that will help an Authority carry forward the work that was started through CAP, enabling many more young people to communicate and socialize.

Examples of some of the aids

- Dynamyte
- Dynavox
- Dynawrite
- Boardmaker
- Mini Mo
- Say it Sam
- Chatbox
- Mighty Mo
- Tellus, Tellus Plus.

Helpful hints

- It is recommended that schools have a 'Communication Policy' and this should cover AAC.
- Parents/carers and the children must be firmly committed throughout the process of assessment and trialing.
- Training and support, for everyone concerned, are important elements in the process and crucial to the successful use of high technology aids.
- Programmes of study in schools must be suitably differentiated to enable each child to access the curriculum according to his or her communication needs.
- Time must be built in to maximize the effectiveness of high technology aids and communication software.
- It is important to identify the support needed to enable the pupil to use the communication aid functionally.
- The support of a technician is useful. This may cover physical adaptation to mounting bars or software management, etc.
- Appoint a named key worker to co-ordinate the use of AAC and pupils' access to the curriculum.
- Review a child's needs on a regular basis, especially where aids are wheelchair mounted.

Communication Aids Project
Becta, Millburn Hill Road, Science Park, Coventry
CV4 7JJ
www.ace-centre.org.uk
http://cap.becta.org.uk

INDIVIDUAL EDUCATION PLAN

Name:	**Area of concern:** Autistic Spectrum Disorder
Year: 1	**Strengths:** Rote memory, interest in cars
Stage:	**Teacher/Support:** LSA x 2 hours per day

Start date:	
Review date:	
IEP no.: 3	

Targets:
1. To sit still and quietly in assembly.
2. To sit on the carpet appropriately during literacy and numeracy.
3. To be the milk monitor for his table.
4. To play constructively with up to 2 peers at playtime.

Strategies for use in class:
1. Always address x by name.
2. Always give clear, simple instructions.
3. Use a visual timetable and task list.
4. Make use of x's interest in cars to make word cards, number lines, etc.
5. Make use of this interest to encourage social interaction.
6. Use this interest to give rewards.
7. Keep to routines – if there is going to be a change prepare x well in advance.
8. Keep interested through a variety of tasks.
9. Make use of x's memory in mental maths.

Role of Parent(s)/Carer(s):
1. Daily contact through 'home/class' book.
2. Daily reading.

Success criteria:
1. Will be able to sit in assembly like his peers.
2. Increasing time spent appropriately, beginning with 5 minutes and escalating.
3. To carry out 'monitor' duties without reminders.
4. To play with LSA supervision in the first instance; LSA gradually withdrawing to a distance.

Resources:
1. A square of carpet for use in assembly and during literacy and numeracy to create a clear boundary.
2. Clear labels on all equipment using pictures and symbols.
3. Visual timetable and task lists.
4. Social stories – see Advisor.
5. Use of spinning tops, skittles, etc. for playtime.

Agreed by:	
SENCO:	
Parent(s)/Carer(s):	
Pupil:	
Date:	

Autistic Spectrum Disorder (ASD)

Autism is a pervasive developmental disorder and since the 1980s the idea of a 'spectrum of autistic disorders' has been widely acknowledged.

The causes of autism are complex and it is unlikely that there is a single cause, but rather a set of triggers involving biological/medical, psychological and behavioural factors. There appears to be a strong genetic link.

Psychological assessments can be helpful but they cannot be used to confirm or deny a diagnosis of Autistic Spectrum Disorder (ASD). The diagnosis is medical and is made by recognizing patterns of behaviour from early life which indicate impairment of social interaction, communication and development of imagination. This is known as the 'triad of impairments'.

At one end of the spectrum will be a normally intelligent child with mild autism, and at the other end will be the child with profound learning difficulties and severe autism. The estimated prevalence of ASD is six in 1,000 and it affects four times as many boys as girls.

The main characteristics

● Social interaction
The child will have an inability to empathize with others and will find it difficult to understand the feelings and/or behaviour of others. He or she may appear withdrawn and make little attempt to make friends, often being described as 'aloof'. Sometimes their behaviour is odd – using inappropriate greetings, touching or being aggressive.

Children with ASD have difficulties understanding and interpreting social situations and may become distressed or confused.

● Communication
This includes a difficulty in making sense of and using both verbal and non-verbal communication such as eye contact, facial expression, gesture and body language.

Some children never develop speech; others experience a significant language delay and when they do begin to use language it is often repetitive and/or learned phrases from things such as television cartoons or adverts.

In contrast, some children appear to have good expressive language but still have difficulties in understanding and tend to interpret literally.

● Thought and imagination
An impairment in thought and imagination affects every area of thinking, language and behaviour.

In Early Years settings an impairment in play and imaginative activities is often noticeable. Children may become fixated by a particular toy, especially one that spins and shines. They may develop repetitive and/or obsessive interests and are often more interested in objects than people.

Changes in routine can cause distress because ASD children are dependent upon routine to make sense of their environment.

Additional difficulties
In addition to the 'triad of impairments', children with ASD may experience any number of the following.

● Hand flapping, rocking or spinning
● Sensitivity to noise, smell, taste, touch or visual stimuli
● Erratic sleeping patterns
● Unusual eating habits
● Self injury
● Aggressive behaviour
● Hyperactivity
● A strange gait or posture – often walking on tip-toes
● Irrational fears or phobias

About 10 per cent have a special creative or mathematical skill such as remembering dates or making complicated mathematical calculations.

How can we help?
● Have a structured classroom – use labels and specific areas for specific tasks.
● Provide an individual work area – acknowledge the need for personal space.
● Use a visual timetable and task lists.
● Consider lighting, noise, etc.
● Introduce only one skill at a time.
● Be positive and patient – keep calm and be flexible.
● Always refer to the child by name – they may not realize 'everyone' includes them.
● Use obsessions as rewards and encourage interaction through activities they enjoy.
● Teach them to recognize behaviours, emotions, body language.
● Do not expect eye contact and never turn their face to look at you.
● Keep verbal instructions brief and simple.
● Use stories to teach social communication/interaction.
● Teach jokes, puns and metaphors.
● Disapprove of inappropriate behaviour, not the child.
● Provide clear boundaries for behaviour.
● Prepare for changes in advance.
● Develop a 'buddy' system.
● Make good use of computers.
● Have high expectations.
● Always talk to parents.

National Autistic Society
email: nas@mailbox.ulcc.ac.uk
www.nas.org.uk

Centre for the Study of Autism:
www.autism.org/contents.html

INDIVIDUAL BEHAVIOUR PLAN

Name:

Year:

Stage:

Area of concern: Disruptive behaviour

Strengths: Good at sport, especially football

Teacher/Support: TA

Start date:

Review date:

IEP no.:

Targets:
1. To remain in seat during all lessons for a whole day.
2. To stay on task for at least 50% of time for the whole week.
3. To not disrupt other pupils while they work.

Strategies for use in class:
1. Seat at front, next to *y*.
2. Praise when on task.
3. TA to build in purposeful breaks during lesson e.g. get dictionary from bookshelf, give out worksheets.
4. Use record card to provide visual recognition of success (10 min slots).

Role of Parent(s)/Carer(s):
1. To keep in touch with school and inform of progess made.
2. To support work of school by providing treats as rewards when appropriate.

Success criteria:
1. Remained in seat when required.
2. Record card shows 50% on task behaviour for week.
3. No recorded instances of disruption for whole week.

Resources:
1. TA to supervise filling in of record card (to be initialled by teacher).
2. Personalized record card.
3. Letter sent to parents at end of week.

Agreed by:

SENCO:

Parent(s)/Carer(s):

Pupil:

Date:

Behavioural, Emotional and Social Difficulties (BESD)

Children considered to have behavioural, emotional and social difficulties often present a far greater challenge to teachers than pupils with other kinds of special needs. The main reason for this is the negative effect they can have on other pupils in the class and the demands they make on the time and energies of the teacher. Pupils who are unco-operative and disruptive form only part of this group, however; others will be withdrawn and uncommunicative and possibly overlooked in terms of support and effective intervention.

Pupils with BESD span the full range of ability and their difficulties can be mild to severe. At the milder end of the continuum, pupils have problems with social interaction and find it difficult to work with others; they do not cope well in unstructured time such as lunch breaks and may have poor concentration in lessons. They may appear quiet and withdrawn and isolated within the group. Other pupils will provoke peers and behave in a confrontational and defiant way. They may be 'off-task' for much of the time and verbally aggressive if reprimanded. Their self-esteem is low and they find it hard to accept any sort of praise or take responsibility for their behaviour. Pupils with more severe difficulties may find it almost impossible to function in a group situation and frequently exhibit violent behaviour which requires physical intervention.

Children with BESD often have learning difficulties and these may result in feelings of frustration and anger which turn into 'bad behaviour'. It is important to look for underlying reasons for this type of situation, such as poor language skills, misunderstanding of social situations (ASD) etc., and put into place strategies to address the root cause of the problem. Conversely, pupils who are very able can become bored in school when work is insufficiently challenging and this can lead to a different kind of frustration that can manifest itself in disruptive behaviour.

The key to effective provision for these pupils is getting to know them and establishing a good relationship with them. This is more difficult for teachers in secondary schools, who spend less time with each pupil than do their primary-school colleagues. Teaching assistants are often an invaluable resource in supporting older pupils, moving with them from subject to subject and creating a good working relationship underpinned by a consistent and sympathetic approach.

General behaviour management

Good behaviour management should be part of every teacher's repertoire of professional skills. This includes the use of voice and body language, questioning skills, sharing attention between all members of a class, modelling good manners and consideration, and adopting appropriate methods of reward and sanctions. Particular strategies are listed below, but perhaps the two most important points to remember are:

- 'Condemn the action, not the child': 'That was a very unkind thing to say to William, it's upset him a lot,' rather than 'You're a very cruel and naughty boy.' Attaching 'bad behaviour' labels to children tends to result in a self-fulfilling situation; you give them a reputation to 'live down to' rather than positive expectations to 'live up to'.
- Catch them being good. Look for opportunities to praise pupils for behaving well. This reinforces good behaviour and is much more powerful than berating them for poor behaviour. Moderate the way in which you do this to suit the age and temperament of the individual (older pupils may not welcome public acclaim, but a word in private – and/or to parents – can be well-received).

Reinforcing good behaviour

Here are some suggestions for praising pupils:

I like the way you got on with your work today and didn't waste time.
You are all listening very well.
Jason, you tried really hard to work out that problem – well done.
The whole class has worked well today – I have enjoyed teaching you.
I noticed how you tried to help Lucy with her work, that was very kind. Thank you.
I saw that Emma was trying to distract you, but you carried on with your work – well done. You set a good example to Emma, and the rest of the class.
That question you asked today was impressive. It told me that you're really thinking about things. Well done.
You dealt very well with that unkind remark from Paul – well done, it was a very mature response.

The ABC of behaviour management

- A – antecedents: situations, conditions which lead to certain behaviours
- B – behaviour: how a child behaves as a result
- C – consequences: the actions taken by the teacher

Antecedents

These are aspects of the situation and environment which lead to the behaviour exhibited.

- **The school's ethos** – does it promote a positive and purposeful atmosphere, where pupils and teachers feel valued and work together in a supportive and safe environment?

- **Teacher behaviour** – are you prepared, organized, welcoming? Do you have a sense of humour and a sense of fun, and show that you enjoy lessons?
- **The curriculum** – is there planned continuity and appropriate progression, with tasks differentiated to match pupils' abilities?
- **The lesson** – do you have:
  - a clear and focused lesson plan?
  - clear and achievable learning objectives for the lesson, shared with pupils?
  - clear and explicit behaviour objectives, shared with the pupils?
- **A pupil's background** – there may be extreme circumstances impacting on an individual's behaviour.
- **In-child factors** – specific medical, psychological or neurological conditions that need to be addressed.

The Four Rs

Rights, rules, routines and responsibilities (the four Rs) should be clearly displayed, regularly referred to and understood by all pupils. They should be written in appropriate terms for the age of the children and refer to:

- understanding the **rights** of others to learn;
- seeing the need for **rules**;
- accepting and conforming to class **routines**;
- taking **responsibility** for one's own behaviour.

Behaviour

The resulting behaviour may be challenging, unacceptable or difficult behaviour expressed in a variety of ways: disrupting the work of other children, shouting out, wandering around the classroom, throwing things, refusing to engage with the task set. Quiet disengagement may go unnoticed, especially if there are other pupils demanding the teacher's attention.

The behaviour may be designed to: gain attention, avoid completing the work, prevent the teacher (and peers) from identifying some difficulty experienced by the child, demonstrate power, seek power, or escape by withdrawing.

Consequences

There will be consequences to inappropriate behaviour, which may be fairly minor or result in extreme and difficult situations. Consequences follow for both teachers and pupils.

Establish a hierarchy of strategies:

- eye contact, move nearer/next to the pupil, non-verbal contact, say the pupil's name;
- question (Is there a problem?), support, offer choice, reminder, redirection (I need you to. . .);
- warning, clarify consequences (If you carry on like this . . . this is what will happen: you have a choice. . .);
- consequences (sanctions): writing pupil's name on the board; making a note in the home/school diary or on the daily report form; time out; keeping pupil in to finish work during break/ lunch; staying after school (detention); report to year tutor/ headteacher/parents.

The underlying approach of the ABC model is to address the antecedents, avoiding the creation of 'triggers' and dealing effectively with undesirable behaviour through effective classroom management.

Positive behaviour management strategies

- Pupil-friendly systems such as 'traffic lights' and noise gauges (teach pupils the use of different voices – for discussion groups, pair work, etc. to prevent too much escalation of noise)
- Catching pupils 'being good' – and giving appropriate praise/ reinforcement
- Tasks matched to pupils' abilities
- Careful consideration of groupings, ensuring that a child with BESD has access to good role models
- Regular breaks incorporated into the lesson – change of pace/ activity; introduce movement, brain gym exercises
- Enhancing the pupil's self-esteem
- Making explicit to pupils the effects of their behaviour
- Being clear about what constitutes unacceptable behaviour; referring regularly to the classroom code of conduct
- Using humour, where appropriate, to deflect anger and avoid confrontation (but avoid humiliating pupils)
- Instigating a 'time out' facility
- Teaching anger-management strategies
- Where possible, fostering and encouraging parental support
- Early identification of learning difficulties and effective support provided
- Controls, restrictions and sanctions that are fair and consistently applied
- Appropriate rewards

INDIVIDUAL EDUCATION PLAN

Name:

Year: 4

Stage:

Area of concern: Cerebral Palsy and mild learning difficulties

Strengths: Determination

Teacher/Support: 15 hours LSA

Start date:

Review date:

IEP no.:

Role of Parent(s)/Carer(s):
1. Regular liaison between home and school – use of 'home/school' book.
2. Help with reading and spelling games, 15 minutes after tea Mon, Tues, Wed, Thur.

Targets:
1. To complete set physiotherapy programme.
2. To complete at least two readers per week.
3. To learn 15 more words from NLS, Year 1–2 (see literacy record book for specifics) for both reading and spelling.
4. To complete the 'core' activities from each lesson.

Strategies for use in class:
1. Ensure x can manoeuvre successfully within the classroom – ensure clutter free aisles.
2. Use a buddy system for help at break, lunch and in PE.
3. Set 'core' targets for completion in lessons (bearing in mind the possible need for extra time).
4. Use a sloping writing desk.
5. Make good use of computer aids – as advised by the OT.
6. Use ALS games for help with reading/spelling tasks.

Success criteria:
1. As assessed by the physiotherapist.
2. Evidence in the reading diary.
3. Successful reading and spelling of the words on at least three occasions.
4. Completion of 'core' activities.

Resources:
1. Advice and help from both the physiotherapist and the OT – see reports.
2. 15 hours LSA time.
3. Computer aids located in x's classroom – see Ms. z for guidance on use.
4. ALS games and multi-sensory learning aids.
5. Sloping desk for writing tasks.

Agreed by:

SENCO:

Parent(s)/Carer(s):

Pupil:

Date:

Cerebral Palsy (CP)

Cerebral Palsy is a general term for a wide range of non-progressive cerebral (brain) disorders. It is a persistent disorder of movement and posture and occurs when part of the brain is not working properly or has not developed. This happens before birth, at birth or during early childhood, in other words before the brain's growth has reached a certain level of maturity. The affected part of the brain usually controls muscles and certain movements and CP results in jumble messages between the brain and the muscles. It is estimated that one in 400 children are affected. No two people with CP are the same and the term covers the full spectrum, from those in whom it is barely noticeable to those who are severely affected.

Types of Cerebral Palsy

Spastic – this is an impairment of the cerebral cortex and is the most common form of CP. Spastic means 'stiff' and those with spastic CP have stiffened muscles and decreased movement in their joints.

- Hemiplegia – one side of the body affected
- Diplegia – legs affected more than arms
- Quadriplegia – arms and legs both affected

Athetoid – an impairment of the basal ganglia. This is where the muscles rapidly change from floppy to tense resulting in involuntary movements. Speech can be hard to understand because those affected have difficulty controlling their tongue, breathing and vocal cords. Hearing problems can also occur.

Ataxic – this is rare and caused by impairment in the cerebellum. Those with ataxic CP find it difficult to balance and have poor spatial awareness. The whole of the body is affected and although they can walk they may be unsteady. In addition they may experience shaky hand movements and jerky speech.

The effects of CP vary so much, it is often difficult to diagnose which type is present: and many people have a combination of types. It is also difficult to predict how a child's independence will be affected in later life. CP is not progressive although some difficulties may become more noticeable as the child gets older. There is no cure but good positioning, early play and physiotherapy can improve posture and muscle control.

Therapy

Therapists and Educational Psychologists play an important part in assessing a child's needs and in advising the best ways of promoting development:

- Speech and Language Therapy
- Occupational Therapy/Physiotherapy
- Conductive Education
- Bobath Therapy
- Botulinum Toxin A.

Associated difficulties

A child with CP may not have any associated difficulties but staff in school need to bear in mind the possibility of problems with:

- sleeping
- constipation
- speech and understanding the spoken word
- epilepsy
- visual perception
- learning difficulties – moderate to severe
- specific learning difficulties (specific parts of the brain affected).

Inclusion

Early school experiences can have a profound effect on how people feel about themselves and influence their expectations about their future role in society. It is important that the education experience is a positive one for all children, but especially those with a disability. Being included, or having regular contact with mainstream peers can improve youngsters' confidence and raise their aspirations. It also means that non-disabled children learn to accept people with 'differences' and how to accommodate them in society.

How can we help?

- Talk to parents.
- Co-ordinate the work of all relevant specialist/therapists.
- Think about physical access – ramps, lifts, toilets, classroom layout.
- Think about curriculum access – teaching styles, learning objectives, appropriate support, allowing extra time.
- Use a 'buddy' system.
- Make use of ICT – the LEA advisor may be able to help (*Inclusive Technology* and *Semerc* are specialist providers).
- Make use of audio-visual aids.
- Promote 'difference' through PSHE.

Remember, someone who is severely physically affected may be of average or above average intelligence!

Scope
6 Market Road,
London N7 9PW
www.scope.org.uk
www.conductive-education.org.uk
tel: 0121 449 1569
www.inclusive.co.uk tel: 01457 819790
www.semerc.com tel: 0161 827 2927

INDIVIDUAL EDUCATION PLAN

Name:

Year: 8

Stage: Statement

Start date:

Review date:

IEP no.: 3

Area of concern: Rhett's Syndrome. Pre-verbal. Behaviour that can be misinterpreted as aggressive. Incontinent. Scoliosis

Strengths: Constantly tries to communicate. Loves water and swimming

Teacher/Support:

Targets:

1. To touch, grasp and hold a variety of objects (not food) for up to 30 seconds.
2. To tolerate foot massage as part of her MOVE programme.
3. To press the 'Big Mack' as appropriate.

Strategies for use in class:

1. Seat in work chair with table attachment. Present with a variety of objects to hold, explore and play with – useful in maths activities. Praise and reward.
2. Encourage sitting and participating in stretches and massage.
3. Modelling, physical help, praise and reward.

Role of Parent(s)/Carer(s):

1. To practise holding at home in similar situations.
2. To provide swimming as a reward following foot massage.
3. Daily liaison through diary.

Success criteria:

1. Will hold an item for 30 seconds on between two and five occasions.
2. Will participate in foot massage on 3/5 occasions.
3. Will press Big Mack on 2/5 occasions with some prompting.

Resources:

1. Specialized chair and attachment. Variety of objects of varying sizes to hold. Reward chart.
2. Massage oils, towel, etc.
3. Big Mack attachment, appropriate software/programs.

Agreed by:

SENCO:

Parent(s)/Carer(s):

Pupil:

Date:

Complex Learning Difficulties

Children described as having complex learning difficulties are not one homogenous group but include those with a combination of any or all of the following:

- severe learning difficulties
- severe behavioural, emotional and/or social difficulties
- severe communication difficulties
- severe sensory, medical and/or physical difficulties.

These children are sometimes described as having profound and multiple learning difficulties.

The prevalence of children with complex difficulties has increased over recent years due in most part to reduced infant mortality rates. The result of an increasing survival rate of premature babies is that the nature of learning difficulties is also becoming more complex. Current prevalence is estimated to be one to two in 1000.

The main characteristics

- Significant cognitive impairment, i.e. learning difficulties
- Speech, language and communication problems
- Organizational problems
- Short attention span
- Lack of social interaction skills
- Limited independent living skills

Children may have problems with:

- Feeding
- Gross motor skills, e.g. walking, skipping
- Fine motor skills, e.g. using a pencil, cutting with scissors
- Behaviour
- Memory
- Personal care, e.g. toileting.

In addition children with complex difficulties are more likely to have a variety of medical needs.

How can we help?

Children with complex difficulties are entitled to a broad and balanced curriculum, including the National Curriculum, like any other child. Skills for life such as mobility, eating and communication will be important features of their education, but these skills can be taught effectively through the various National Curriculum areas. It is becoming increasingly common for these pupils to have contact with mainstream schools, perhaps through part-time placements or regular visits. They will usually have a support assistant accompanying them, but the teacher of the class they are joining will be responsible for the learning taking place during any particular session and should plan accordingly. An understanding of P-levels will be essential for this.

Staff roles within a classroom must be clear and information sharing is vital. All children with complex difficulties will have individual targets and possibly a care plan with which the class teacher should be familiar.

- Set small, achievable goals.
- Use multi-sensory stimulus – be sure to include all the senses. Some schools will have sensory rooms or 'corners' and these can be particularly effective in helping children with complex difficulties to shut out external stimulus and channel their attention.
- Enlist the help of other pupils in the class – make sure that they understand the difficulties experienced by a child with complex needs.
- Make experiences practical and relevant.
- Be flexible.
- Talk with any therapists involved with the child and ensure that therapy goals dovetail with learning goals.
- Make communication a goal in every activity.
- Use over-learning techniques.
- Make use of technology – choosing appropriate technology requires a thorough knowledge of the individual's needs and capabilities.
- Ensure labels are clear and provided in both words and symbols.
- Be consistent.
- Ensure the classroom is safe – this can be difficult when a number of special chairs and items of equipment have to be kept at hand.
- If possible, organize the room so that specific activities are associated with specific areas.
- Be patient!

Remember!

- Always work in partnership with parents.

INDIVIDUAL EDUCATION PLAN

Name:

Year: 8

Stage:

Area of concern: Organizational difficulties, Social skills

Strengths: Individual work, with clear targets

Teacher/Support: LSA for two hours every day

Start date:

Review date:

IEP no.:

Targets:

1. To arrive at lessons with appropriate books and equipment.
2. To buy and eat lunch in the dining hall with one of three 'buddies'.
3. To contribute to group work in English lessons.

Strategies for use in class:

1. Remember to praise x for bringing the appropriate books and equipment to lessons (and write a comment in his Personal Work Record).
2. Make sure he writes in his PWR appropriate reminders for next lesson (e.g. ingredients for food technology).
3. Give x clear targets for each lesson (these may be different to those for other pupils in terms of length of pieces of writing, etc.).
4. Encourage x to work with other pupils as well as his LSA. As he prefers to work on his own, offer this opportunity as an incentive, 'Work with b on this experiment and talk to him about what happens; then you can fill in the work sheet on your own'.
5. In group work, ensure that x has a clear role within the group and understands what is expected of him.

Role of Parent(s)/Carer(s):

1. To check x PWR every day and ensure that a) homework is completed on time, b) books/equipment are ready for the following day.
2. To allow x to bring home a friend after school one evening per week.
3. To pass on to x any positive feedback from staff.

Success criteria:

1. To increase the number of positive comments from subject teachers in x's Personal Work Record (Currently two from a possible 25).
2. To be seen sitting with other pupils in the dining hall and eating lunch in an acceptable manner.
3. To accept a given role within a group in English lessons, and (with support from LSA) to contribute to the joint effort.

Resources:

1. Wherever possible, inform the LSA of work to be covered in the next lesson – she may design an alternative worksheet or method of recording.
2. x to see the SENCO every day before afternoon registration, to discuss his lunchtime behaviour and give positive reinforcement where appropriate.
3. Attendance at the lunchtime study club to read with a 'buddy', play spelling games, etc.

Agreed by:

SENCO:

Parent(s)/Carer(s):

Pupil:

Date:

Down's Syndrome

Down's Syndrome is a genetic disorder and occurs when a baby is born with an additional chromosome (47 instead of 46). It is the most common form of learning disability, occurring in about one of every 1000 live births a year. Children with Down's Syndrome are not just generally delayed in their development: they have a specific learning profile with characteristic strengths and weaknesses.

Many schools are now welcoming children with Down's Syndrome into the mainstream and increased involvement with their non-disabled peers, coupled with higher expectations from teachers, means that children are achieving far more – both socially and educationally.

The main characteristics

There are specific physical features associated with the condition and children may have problems such as eye defects, respiratory problems and heart defects. Learning difficulties range from moderate to severe.

The following factors are typical of many children with Down's Syndrome. Some have physical implications, others have cognitive ones; some have both.

- Delayed motor skills – fine and gross
- Auditory and visual impairment
- Speech and language impairment
- Poor auditory memory
- Limited concentration span
- Difficulties with thinking and reasoning, and applying knowledge to new situations
- Sequencing difficulties

Like all children with special needs, those with Down's Syndrome need to be treated as individuals. There is a wide variety of measurable ability within this group, which makes generalization difficult. Many children grow up to lead independent lives within their community, holding down a job and enjoying a lasting relationship.

How can we help?

There is no definitive guide to good practice and teachers are often confused about how to respond to these youngsters in the classroom. Often, they link inappropriate behaviour to the child's label and believe that it can't be challenged or managed; the tendency is to be over-protective and lenient.

Working alongside parents, sharing practice and experience with colleagues and involving the youngsters themselves in planning and decision-making constitute the foundation of good provision.

- Nominate a key person in school to be the first point of contact if there is a problem.
- Teach timetable, routines and school rules explicitly, allowing time to learn them.
- Make sure the rules are clear and apply them to pupils with Down's syndrome alongside their peers.
- Speak directly to the pupil and reinforce what you say with facial expression, pictures and concrete materials.
- Use simple and familiar language and short sentences.
- Give the child time to process language and form a response.
- Listen carefully – your ear will adjust.
- Ensure consistency of approach by all teachers and non-teaching staff.
- Use short, clear instructions and check understanding.
- Provide additional practice to develop motor skills.
- Distinguish the 'can't do' from the 'won't do'.
- Consider any inappropriate behaviour in terms of 'why did this happen?' Check whether.
  - the pupil understands the task
  - the task is too hard or too easy
  - the materials used are too babyish
  - the task is too long.
- For a younger child, make an activity box for times when he finishes an activity before his peers or needs a change of task or 'time out'. Put in books, fine-motor skills activities, etc. Allow another child to join in as a way of encouraging social interaction.
- Provide lots of short listening activities and use visual/tactile materials to reinforce oral work.
- Set up regular and frequent opportunities for the pupil to speak to others (both peers and adults).
- Ignore attention-seeking behaviour within reasonable limits.
- Remember that the class teacher has ultimate responsibility for the child (the LSA should not be the only adult dealing with him or her).
- Be aware that too much one-to-one support can be counter-productive.
- Make sure the pupil is working with others who are good role models.

Down's Syndrome Association
Landgon Down Centre,
2a Langdon Park,
Teddington,
TW11 9PS Tel: 0845 230 0372
www.downs-syndrome.org.uk

INDIVIDUAL EDUCATION PLAN

Name:

Year: 3

Stage:

Area of concern: Dyscalculia

Strengths: Art, oral work, reading

Teacher/Support: LSA for Numeracy & Science groups

Start date:

Review date:

IEP no.: 2

Targets:

1. To be able to name a triangle, rectangle and hexagon.
2. To be able to compute numbers up to 20 using addition and subtraction.
3. To be able to make a simple tally chart.
4. To answer at least one question during the oral part of the Numeracy hour.

Strategies for use in class:

1. Use multi-sensory learning methods concentrating on just one shape at a time and do not move on until that shape is secure.
2. Make sure the calculations are written in x's book in advance; leave a clear space between and put a green dot above the units column to remind x that this is where to start. Ensure that concrete apparatus is available.
3. Use the computer program. On paper encourage the use of different colours. Make sure that when first teaching, the concrete example is available.
4. Ask the same question of another member of the class directly before x. As x becomes more confident leave a gap. Always make sure the question is within the work x has covered.

Role of Parent(s)/Carer(s):

1. To play the Snakes & Ladders Shape Game.
2. Encourage x to see numbers in everyday life – booklet provided with suggestions.

Success criteria:

1. Successfully naming these shapes on at least three separate occasions.
2. Consistent success with computations.
3. For x to be able to make a simple tally chart without assistance.
4. For x to feel comfortable answering questions during the oral session (demonstrated by volunteering answers).

Resources:

1. Group work with the LSA during Numeracy Hour and one Science session if needed.
2. Concrete shapes to feel and draw around, various worksheets, jigsaws, sand tray, computer program, the Snakes & Ladders Shape Game, dice.
3. LSA time to write calculations in x's book in advance. Use of Cuisennaire or cubes as preferred by x.
4. Computer program, box of resources for concrete apparatus, boxes of pasta, coloured pens/pencils.

Agreed by:

SENCO:

Parent(s)/Carer(s):

Pupil:

Date:

Dyscalculia

Dyscalculia is one of a group of specific learning difficulties. It is a specific learning disability in mathematics. It should not be confused with dyslexia, which is a difficulty with words. In fact, students can be gifted in other academic areas but be confounded by maths.

What are the causes?

There are several possibilities that have been put forward for the causes of dyscalculia, including problems that occur at the foetal stage so that part of the brain is not 'wired up' correctly. In addition it has been acknowledged that fear and poor instruction could also play a large part.

Types

There are two main types of dyscalculia:

Developmental Dyscalculia – this is where there is a marked discrepancy between a person's developmental level and general cognitive ability on measures of specific maths ability.

Dyscalculia – a total inability to abstract or consider concepts and numbers.

The main characteristics

It will take some observation and gathering of evidence to imply that dyscalculia is the problem rather than a single mathematical concept that has not been grasped. Difficulties may include the following.

- An inability to learn to count by rote
- Difficulty reading and/or writing numbers
- Inconsistent computation results
- Omissions
- Reversals
- Transpositions
- Poor mental maths
- An inability to grasp and remember mathematical concepts, rules and formulae
- Difficulty with time and time management
- Problems with sequencing – this can affect many things, including problems with team games and dance sequences
- Poor sense of direction
- Poor memory for lay-out
- Confusion with left and right
- Stress at lesson change-over times
- Difficulties with games – they may lose track of whose turn it is
- Inability to remember names or faces
- Difficulties with money

There are a number of specific tests that can be used to identify dyscalculia and the Educational Psychologist should be able to help with this in school.

How can we help?

As with most strategies used to help those with special needs, these approaches will benefit all pupils.

- The first thing to do is find out what type of learner they are: grasshopper or inchworm.
- Ask a child to explain how they have come to an answer – sometimes it may seem a little bizarre but if they understand it that way and it is mathematically workable, accept this.
- Always explain a new concept step-by-step.
- Encourage the child to teach it back to check they have understood.
- Use concrete apparatus (some children may never move from this stage): these days there is a wealth of material that can be purchased, from bright plastic pies for teaching fractions to large dice for playing games.
- Use picture and visual stimuli.
- Use multi-sensory methods – e.g. use the sand tray to trace numbers just as you would letters – make maths as practical as possible.
- Carefully teach the language and syntax of maths.
- Use number stories.
- Encourage spaces between sums on a page – make sure the work is uncluttered and clearly set out.
- If there is a problem copying numbers down accurately either from a book or the board make sure these are already in the children's book or folder.
- Make use of the computer.
- Make use of a calculator – some children may always struggle so we must encourage and teach them to use the tools that can do the job for them.
- Acknowledge the trauma that these children experience with maths.
- Allow extra time – this will be important in stressful times such as tests or examinations.
- Encourage the use of rough paper to work out calculations.
- Use wall displays with each of the four symbols in the middle and all the words used to mean that around the outside.
- For older pupils, use a credit card holder to keep reminders of formulae, tables, etc.
- Make good use of mnemonics to help remember sequences, e.g. 'Damned Silly Triangle'.
- Encourage peer support for getting round the school, changing lessons, etc.
- For older pupils, ensure someone will help with organization at exam time.

www.dyscalculia.co.uk

INDIVIDUAL EDUCATION PLAN

Name:

Year: 4

Stage:

Area of concern: Writing

Strengths: Good oral skills. Imaginative

Teacher/Support: TA

Start date:

Review date:

IEP no.: 1

Role of Parent(s)/Carer(s):
1. To encourage short writing tasks at home – shopping lists, birthday cards, etc.
2. To share in cutting-out and colouring activities to improve fine motor control.

Targets:
1. To improve pencil grip.
2. To complete creative writing tasks in Literacy lesson.
3. To produce more legible writing.

Strategies for use in class:
1. Mrs z to present x with a number of different pens, pencils and moulded grips to find out which is most comfortable and easy to use.
2. Mrs z to support x in getting down his ideas for stories. Extra time to be allowed for completion of work as appropriate.
3. Predictive text software to be used for final draft of stories.
4. Letter formation practised for ten minutes everyday (using school scheme).

Success criteria:
1. Writing with a more comfortable grip that gives greater pencil control and does not cause discomfort.
2. To hand in a completed piece of creative work at least once a week.
3. Letters written with correct orientation and shape.

Resources:
1. Assorted pens and pencils, grips, paper with wide lines.
2. Software: Penfriend, Clicker.
3. Handwriting practice sheets.

Agreed by:

SENCO:

Parent(s)/Carer(s):

Pupil:

Date:

Dysgraphia

Dysgraphia is a Latin word. *Dys* means 'difficulty with'; *graphia* refers to the writing process. More precisely, dysgraphia is a difficulty with the neurological processing needed to write letters, words or numbers with ease. It affects people in varying degrees, ranging from mild to moderate. Dysgraphia may exist in isolation but more commonly occurs with other learning difficulties, like dyslexia, aphasia, dyscalculia and attention deficit disorder.

Difficulty with writing often leads to major misunderstandings by teachers and parents, and consequently to many frustrations for the student. This is especially true for bright, linguistically competent pupils who struggle with written expression due to their lack of smooth, efficient automaticity in letter and word formation. They cannot easily demonstrate in writing what they know and understand, and so teachers may underestimate their abilities. All too often, the child's difficulty is interpreted as poor motivation, carelessness, laziness, or excessive speed. While these circumstances may well contribute to the problem, the underlying cause may be dysgraphia, which is not within the child's control.

The main characteristics

Specific symptoms which may be noted include the folbuing.

- Cramped fingers and awkward pen/pencil grip
- Odd wrist, body and paper positions
- Mixture of upper and lower case letters
- Mixture of printed and cursive letters
- Inconsistent letter formations and slant
- Irregular letter sizes and shapes
- Unfinished letters
- Reversing letters/numbers
- Writing letters out of order
- Misuse of line and margin
- Poor organization on the page
- Slowness in both copying and independent writing
- General illegibility, with frequent erasures/corrections
- Reliance on vision to monitor what the hand is doing during writing
- Slowness in implementing verbal directions that involve sequencing and planning

How can we help?

Dysgraphia can be overcome if appropriate strategies are taught well and conscientiously carried out, preferably on a daily basis.

- In many situations, alternatives to writing can be employed such as making audio/video recordings of a child's verbal or practical work, or using voice recognition software or an amanuensis.
- Be understanding about a child's difficulties and inconsistent performance.
- Allow the pupil to use either print or cursive writing.

- Explore the usefulness of aids such as pencil grips (to hold the pen/pencil correctly), templates (to keep paper in the right place/angle), pre-formed letter shapes (children follow with their finger), sloping board/table top. Experiment with different writing tools and types of paper.
- Provide opportunities and encouragement for regular practice – daily if possible.
  - Practise letter formation in sand/salt trays.
  - Use chalk or coloured marker pens to practise letter formation on black/white board.
  - Practise shape and pattern copying, tracing, colouring by number, following the line to find out which rabbit belongs to which hutch, etc. and threading activities.
- Encourage the use of word processing on a computer. Explore useful software such as predictive text and 'Clicker' grids.
- Teach keyboard skills.
- Encourage the use of a spellchecker.
- Teach editing and proofing skills.
- Allow extra time for writing activities and where possible, accept shorter pieces.
- Teach strategies for organizing thoughts and planning the content prior to writing (e.g. mindmapping).

It is very important to get the main ideas down on paper without having to worry about neatness or the details of spelling. Encourage the children to do the following.

- Use a drafting book and write down just one key word or phrase for each paragraph, then go back later to fill in the details.
- Draw a picture of a thought for each paragraph.
- Dictate ideas into a tape recorder then listen and write them down later.
- Talk to him or herself while writing. This may provide valuable auditory feedback.

If spelling is a problem, encourage children to do the following.

- Look at the word, close their eyes and visualize how it looks, letter by letter.
- Spell the word out loud while looking at it, then look away and spell it out loud again several times before writing it down.
- Use letter tiles or plastic letters and keep rearranging the letters until they look right.

National Handwriting Association
12 Isis Avenue, Bicester, Oxon. OX26 2GS
www.nha-handwriting.org.uk

British Dyslexia Association
Tel: 0118 966 8271
www.bda-dyslexia.org.uk

INDIVIDUAL EDUCATION PLAN

Name:

Year: 8

Stage:

Start date:

Review date:

IEP no.: 2

Area of concern: Dyslexia/SpLD

Strengths: Oral work, art, D&T

Teacher/Support:

Targets:

1. To be able to use syllabification to aid spelling of 10 regular words.
2. To learn to use mind maps for recording and revision.
3. To remember correct books, equipment, etc. for lessons.

Strategies for use in class:

1. Provide key word lists for each subject.
2. Encourage alternative methods of recording/revising, e.g. mind maps.
3. Use x's strengths to explore understanding.
4. Help to make sure x has his/her homework recorded correctly – encourage buddy system.
5. Remember to allow extra time!
6. Praise for having appropriate books and equipment.

Role of Parent(s)/Carer(s):

1. Encourage with organization and homework – visual reminders on door and in bedroom.
2. Ten minutes three times a week to go through spellings.

Success criteria:

1. Can demonstrate syllabification to aid spelling of six regular words on three separate occasions.
2. Can explain and demonstrate how to use mind maps.
3. Has correct books and equipment for all lessons – as recorded by subject teachers on record sheet provided.

Resources:

1. Alpha to Omega, jigwords, etc. for use in spelling sessions.
2. Information sheet on mind maps.
3. Credit card holder for key words.
4. Visual reminder for timetable and organization.
5. Tick sheet for teachers to record x having correct books, etc. in lessons.

Agreed by:

SENCO:

Parent(s)/Carer(s):

Pupil:

Date:

Dyslexia

The literal translation of the word 'dyslexia' is 'difficulty with words'. It can affect an individual's ability to read quickly and efficiently and nearly always results in poor or 'bizarre' spellings. Pupils with dyslexia often have poor short-term memory and difficulty with sequencing and processing information – skills which are important for effective learning in a busy classroom.

There has been a great deal of research and numerous attempts to define dyslexia. The British Dyslexia Association (BDA) defines it as 'a complex neurological condition which is constitutional in origin . . .'. Magnetic Resonance Imaging (MRI) has been used to identify specific areas of the brain involved in reading and preliminary results indicate less activity in certain areas in people with dyslexia. Dyslexia is perhaps best summed up as a syndrome with a wide range of possible causes and symptoms. Although found across the whole range of cognitive ability, the idea that dyslexia presents itself as a discrepancy between expected outcomes and performance is still widely held.

Numbers vary according to the definitions used, but it is generally accepted that between 5 and 10 per cent of the population is affected to some degree. Many dyslexics may be helped through systematic hard work and appropriate interventions, especially when identified early.

The main characteristics

Reading

Many dyslexics describe a page of print as moving or swirling and experience tracking difficulties, frequently losing their place. Poor phonological processing leads to difficulties with blending and segmenting. It can be frustrating to listen to a dyslexic read as they may make frequent errors with high frequency words but seem able to cope with those that are more complicated. Some believe this is because they need to visualize as they read and many of the high-frequency words (the, and, when) do not lend themselves to easy visualization. Whilst many dyslexic children learn to read at a functional level, they remain slow and the activity requires a great deal of effort.

Writing

The written work of dyslexics is often of a poor standard compared with their oral ability. Their work can appear messy, with frequent crossings out and several attempts at a single word. They tend to confuse similar letter shapes such as b/d/p/q, m/w, n/u, and often make anagrams of words, e.g. tired/tried. Early spelling attempts can be 'bizarre' and this usually remains an area of difficulty into adult life.

General difficulties

- Speed of processing
- Poor short-term memory
- Sequencing
- Organization
- Tiredness
- Uneven performance profile
- Behaviour – often a result of frustration

Strengths

Research has come up with a list of attributes that many dyslexics appear to have in greater abundance than non-dyslexics. This includes some form of creativity, whether it is in the form of art, drama, music or architecture. Others excel in individual sports such as swimming and many are known for their powers of lateral thinking.

How can we help?

- Work from their areas of strength.
- Use a multi-sensory programme of teaching and learning.
- Make use of pictures, plans, flow charts.
- Pictorial timetables can be a great help.
- Use videos, tapes and dictaphones and encourage alternative ways of recording.
- Make use of ICT – voice recognition software can be a boon.
- Teach study skills from an early age – the use of mind-maps has proved particularly successful.
- Provide key word lists and displays.
- Encourage the use of line trackers, bookmarks and/or coloured overlays as appropriate.
- Keep board work to a minimum.
- Tackle spelling patterns using methods such as Simultaneous Oral Spelling.
- Teach a structured, cumulative phonic programme.
- Allow sufficient time for all activities.
- Use lots of praise.
- Ensure it is a whole school issue!

Each individual is unique and the key to success lies in teaching on the basis of individual needs and individual preferences.

British Dyslexia Association
Tel: 0118 966 8271 www.bda-dyslexia.org.uk

Dyslexia Institute/Dyslexia Action
Tel: 01784 222 300 www.dyslexia-inst.org.uk

INDIVIDUAL EDUCATION PLAN

Name:

Year: 1

Stage:

Area of concern: Dyspraxia

Strengths: Keen to do well

Teacher/Support:

Start date:

Review date:

IEP no.:

Targets:

1. To use and understand prepositions: in, behind, on, under.
2. To get dressed after PE on her own.
3. To take turns in a game with one other pupil.
4. To establish a pencil grip.

Strategies for use in class:

1. Give clear, short instructions.
2. Arrange a buddy system.
3. Have a card showing the order for getting dressed.
4. Use lots of practical activities such as peg-boards, painting, etc.
5. Make sure seating is correct – feet must be on the ground.
6. Have a range of pencil grips, chunky crayons and pencils for use.
7. Use gentle reminders to keep on task.
8. Use green/red dots to remind which way to work across the page.

Role of Parent(s)/Carer(s):

1. To encourage x to dress herself in the morning.
2. To help with using cutlery.
3. To reinforce work on prepositions (e.g. read books like *Where Is Spot?*, ask x to look 'behind' the sofa for hidden toys, etc. [Hide and seek games])

Success criteria:

1. Can demonstrate use of and understanding of the words on at least three separate occasions.
2. Gets clothes on in the right order.
3. Can play co-operatively with another pupil with at least three different games and on at least five different occasions.
4. Using a consistent grip and hand.

Resources:

1. Sloping board for desk.
2. A variety of pencil grips, pencils, etc.
3. Large arrows on walls to remind her which way to go, e.g. from peg to classroom.
4. 'Language Gap' games.
5. Fifteen minutes three times per week to work on language programme.
6. Carpet square to help positioning for literacy and numeracy hours.

Agreed by:

SENCO:

Parent(s)/Carer(s):

Pupil:

Date:

Dyspraxia (Developmental Coordination Disorder)

Dyspraxia is an immaturity in the way the brain processes information, resulting in messages not being properly transmitted. Children with dyspraxia may have problems with co-ordinating their movements (in some cases, this extends to difficulties in co-ordinating the mouth and tongue, resulting in speech impairment), perception and thought.

Approximately one in 20 children have the condition to some degree, with boys affected four times more frequently than girls.

The main characteristics

The signs of dyspraxia are often noticed by parents early on and may include problems with:

- achieving normal milestones such as sitting up, crawling, walking
- ability to concentrate
- picking up small objects
- language acquisition
- doing a jigsaw or sorting game
- holding a pencil
- understanding spatial concepts of in/on/behind, etc.

In the classroom, the child with dyspraxia will come across numerous difficulties:

- games lessons (particularly where throwing and catching are involved), and music and movement classes

- following sequential instructions
- getting dressed, tying laces
- handwriting
- using a knife and fork
- confusion with laterality, with the child changing between left and right hands
- an inability to recognize potential danger: e.g. jumping from the top of the climbing frame, or for older pupils, using bunsen burners and other equipment in science and technology.

In addition, children may demonstrate general irritability and limited social skills; they may tire easily and need periods of rest. Older pupils may have poor posture and limited body awareness, moving awkwardly and seeming clumsy.

How can we help?

- Give extra supervision and encouragement to stay on task.
- Give clear and unambiguous instructions and check the pupil's understanding (dyspraxic children may not understand sarcasm or irony).
- Make sure that the child's seating allows him or her to rest both feet on the floor, with the desk or table at elbow height and, ideally, with the facility for a sloping surface to work on.
- Position the child with a direct view of the teacher and minimal distractions.
- Limit the amount of handwriting expected by providing printed sheets or offering alternative means of recording.
- Where pen and paper have to be used, try attaching the paper to the desk so that it does not have to be held still.
- Break down activities into small steps.
- Limit the amount of copying from the board; when necessary, use colours and appropriate 'chunking' to help then follow the text.
- Allow extra time for finishing work.
- Teach the pupil strategies to help remember things and to be able to organize him or herself.
- Be aware that growth spurts may accentuate problems.
- In games and outdoor activities be sensitive to the child's limitations and allocate a position/activity which offers the best chance of success.
- Encourage a partner relationship with another child who can help with tricky situations.
- Give extra praise and encouragement.

With appropriate support and encouragement, dyspraxic children can do very well at school; talk to the parents – they may have found their own solutions to many of the problems.

Dyspraxic Foundation
8 West Alley, Hitchin, herts SG5 1EG
Tel: 01462 454986
www.dyspraxiafoundation.org.uk

INDIVIDUAL EDUCATION PLAN

Name:

Year: 3

Stage:

Area of concern: Fragile X Syndrome

Strengths: Reading (though mechanical)

Teacher/Support: LSA

Start date:

Review date:

IEP no.:

Targets:

1. To line up quietly for dinner.
2. To remain seated for 10 minute intervals.
3. To learn to take turns with one or two other children in a game.
4. To be able to add and take away tens and units.

Strategies for use in class:

1. Arrange for x to be first in the line accompanied by LSA. When achieved try another position in line but prepare first.
2. Use star charts, visual prompts, keep to same place in class – preferably quiet with only two or three other children close by and near to the teacher.
3. Work with LSA in small group using various literacy and numeracy games, including working at the computer.
4. Start from success point – see records, use practical apparatus.
5. Be firm but use lots of praise and rewards.
6. Use of quiet place for time out.

Role of Parent(s)/Carer(s):

1. Regular liaison with class teacher.
2. Reinforce quiet times.
3. Play games with Grandma for 10 minutes every Monday and Wednesday after school.

Success criteria:

1. Demonstrating lining up quietly with the LSA.
2. Begin with achieving twice in two sessions a day and build up gradually.
3. To play literacy and numeracy games in a small group.
4. To complete written tasks.

Resources:

1. Playing card-size visual prompts for lining up, sitting still, putting up hand, sitting quietly in assembly.
2. Lotto, Fishing, Dice, Diennes, etc. for games.
3. Star charts, certificates.
4. A quiet corner for respite.

Agreed by:

SENCO:

Parent(s)/Carer(s):

Pupil:

Date:

Fragile X Syndrome

Fragile X Syndrome is the most common form of inherited learning disability, and is caused by a defect in the X chromosome. It is a strongly heritable condition with the possibility that an affected gene may become more affected as it is passed on from one generation to the next. The range of effects is wide and it is not possible to predict from a diagnosis of Fragile X which features a child will show or to what degree he or she will be affected in terms of intellectual impairment and emotional and behavioural problems.

Fragile X can affect males and females, and both can be carriers. It is estimated that one in 3000 is affected and males are more often, and typically more severely, affected than females. Many Fragile X children and adults remain undiagnosed.

The main characteristics

● Early years

In the early years, children with Fragile X may be 'floppy' and developmental milestones may be delayed. Gross and fine motor co-ordination remain poor and this affects handwriting.

● Speech and language

Children who have Fragile X may have clear, relevant language or no language at all. They may suffer from difficulties with sound articulation and/or fluency. This in turn can lead to rapid speech rates, use of jargon and a litany-like phraseology. You may often hear them repeat the last word or phrase spoken to them or that they have spoken themselves. Conversation can be strained as they may frequently digress.

● Cognitive development

The verbal skills of children with Fragile X tend to be better than their reasoning skills. These strengths can lead to relative strengths in other areas such as reading. However, the difficulties with reasoning may mean that number concepts and processes present a problem area.

● Behaviour

This can range from a little impulsivity to disruptive outbursts and over activity. Children may rush around being unable to settle for long at any one activity, and often act without thinking. At times of stress, a child may show anxiety through obsessions such as hand-flapping and can be persistent in his or her attention-seeking.

● Emotional factors

Children with Fragile X do not generally like 'busy' environments and they can be easily overwhelmed. They may find noises and smells upsetting and may react emotionally to relatively minor upsets. They can be over-sensitive to imagined criticism and have a need for security, routine and constant reassurance.

How can we help?

We can lessen anxieties of children who have Fragile X syndrome and improve their performance by looking at what situations we put them in and ensuring any intervention is related to the child's needs.

- Work with parents. Share ideas and strategies with them.
- Use straightforward language/instructions.
- Teach from the point the child has reached and make goals realistic.
- Make the learning situation clear and uncluttered.
- Keep to routines as far as possible and make sure any changes are prepared for and explained.
- Aims and outcomes must be clear to the child.
- Set positive objectives for change when dealing with behaviour.
- Nip bad habits and/or obsessions in the bud.
- Demands must be enforced.
- Use lots of positive feedback and praise, making it clear that you are rewarding a particular behaviour.
- Keep records, so that successful strategies can be revisited and shared with other staff.

The key to effective intervention is the context in which the child lives: 'significant adults' – parents and carers, teachers and support assistants, need to work with consistency in promoting change and development in the child.

Fragile X Society (UK)
Tel: 01424 813147
www.fragilex.org.uk

National Fragile X Foundation (USA)
www.nfxf.org

FRAXA Research Foundation (USA)
www.fraxa.org

INDIVIDUAL EDUCATION PLAN

Name:

Year: 3

Stage:

Area of concern: Hearing, literacy

Strengths: Maths, science, ICT

Teacher/Support:

Start date:

Review date:

IEP no.:

Targets:
1. To sit near the teacher/LSA.
2. To be able to distinguish between words ending in p/b/t/d.
3. To be able to spell c-v-c words ending in p/b/d/t.
4. To read to an adult on a daily basis – in addition to work in the literacy hour.

Strategies for use in class:
1. Always say x's name before asking a question.
2. Try to face x when speaking to him.
3. Try to keep background noise to a minimum whenever possible.
4. Give short instructions, have visual reminders whenever possible.
5. Make sure x always sits near the front for whole class situations.

Role of Parent(s)/Carer(s):
1. To hear x read at least three times per week.
2. To help with spellings.
3. To contact school whenever hearing is affected by colds, etc.

Success criteria:
1. To sit near the teacher/LSA without being reminded.
2. To demonstrate 95% success on at least three separate occasions.
3. As above.
4. Reading diary that shows this has been accomplished.

Resources:
1. Various games including 'Thump the sound', 'Post boxes', etc.
2. Letter frames for c-v-c words and plastic letters.
3. A variety of workbooks.
4. Letter fans.
5. Reading buddies.
6. LSA for 10 minutes three times per week to do specific work on sound discrimination.
7. ALS group.

Agreed by:

SENCO:

Parent(s)/Carer(s):

Pupil:

Date:

Glue Ear

As many as four out of five children have at least one bout of glue ear before their fourth birthday. A substantial number experience regular, recurring symptoms throughout the primary years. These children will benefit from their teachers and parents knowing about the steps they can take to minimize the effects of glue ear.

What is glue ear?

Glue ear occurs when fluid collects in the middle ear space of one or both ears. This often happens after a cold or an infection in the ear or throat, when bacteria get into the middle ear and cause an inflammation of its lining. The Eustachian tubes can become blocked with mucus, making thing worse. The cells from the lining of the middle ear start to use up the remaining air, reducing the pressure in the middle ear space and allowing fluid to fill up the space. The fluid is often quite thin and runny but may become thicker, like glue, and prevent the ear-drum moving freely, resulting in temporary hearing loss.

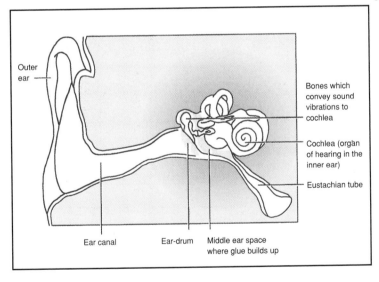

Outer ear

Bones which convey sound vibrations to cochlea

Cochlea (organ of hearing in the inner ear)

Eustachian tube

Ear canal   Ear-drum   Middle ear space where glue builds up

The main characteristics

Children with glue ear experience differing degrees of hearing loss, from mild to severe, and their condition may change from day to day. Teachers and parents should watch out for the following indications.

- Children who are inattentive, appearing to hear 'only when they want to'
- Children who are talking more loudly than usual or talking less and becoming detached

- Children turning up the sound control on TV, audio player or computer
- Saying 'pardon?' or 'what?' more than usual
- Failing to hear a sound which comes from outside their field of vision
- Children experiencing discomfort or pain as a result of an infection in the ear
- Children who are quiet and withdrawn as a result of poor hearing
- Young children may become very tired by the end of the day because of the extra effort required to concentrate on what is being said

What can be done?

For about half the children who have glue ear, symptoms clear up naturally within three months; for others, a visit to the doctor may be necessary. If glue ear is a recurring problem, the child may be referred to an Ear, Nose and Throat specialist (ENT) and/or an audiologist. In severe cases, the specialist may advise putting in grommets. These are miniature ventilation tubes which keep the middle ear aired and healthy. Grommets improve hearing immediately and usually stay in place for between six months and a year. When they come out, the small hole in the ear-drum should heal quickly.

How can we help?

- Attract the child's attention by calling his or her name – *before* asking a question or giving an instruction.
- Talk face to face when possible, sitting or bending to the same level for one-to-one exchange.
- In a whole-class teaching situation, seat the child at the front where he or she can see your face clearly.
- Speak up but don't shout.
- Cut down background noise where possible.
- Keep instructions short and simple.
- When you are sure about a child's hearing loss, explain to classmates how they can help.

(There are particular implications for the phonics element of the Literacy Hour; the teacher will need to ensure that the child is hearing an appropriate sound during sound-symbol work especially. It may be necessary to re-visit this sort of work once the glue ear has cleared up, perhaps with the help of a classroom assistant.)

For an information leaflet on glue ear, contact
Defeating Deafness (Hearing Research Trust)
330-332 Gray's Inn Rd, London WC1X 8EE
Tel: 020 7833 1733

Communication with a Hearing Impaired Child

- Step forward 'out of the crowd' to make it easy for the child to focus on you.

- Speak clearly and at a moderate pace; do not shout. Avoid over-pronunciation or exaggeration.

- Look in the direction of the child.

- Do not stand with your back to the light.

- Avoid blocking visual access to your face – either by hand movements or by holding a book in a way which obscures your face. It is harder for the child to communicate with a person who has a beard and/or wears glasses, as these can 'mask' the facial expression.

- Use 'natural' body language to enhance instructions and explanations.

- Make sure that lighting is adequate to allow the child to see facial expressions clearly.

- Give plenty of context clues when introducing a new subject – start with something which is familiar to the child.

- In a group or class discussion, control the pace and be prepared to repeat points for the child with a hearing impairment.

- Short phrases and sentences are easier to understand than single words.

- Try to reduce the general noise within the classroom and seat the child away from traffic noise, or the hum of the overhead projector.

- Present one source of information at a time. It is difficult for a child with hearing loss to focus on what you are saying at the same time as looking at a book or watching what you are writing on the board.

- Phrase questions to the child carefully and always say his or her name beforehand.

- Obtain feedback from the child at regular intervals – without drawing too much attention to him.

Hearing Impairment

The term 'hearing impairment' is a generic term used to describe all hearing loss. The two terms most used by teachers of the deaf to describe hearing impairment are the 'type' and 'degree' of loss.

Types of loss

The main types of hearing loss are:

Monaural: hearing loss in one ear only. This condition is relatively easy to cope with in the classroom if the teacher is aware of the child's 'good side' and can position him or her appropriately.

Conductive loss: the mechanism by which sound waves reach the nerve endings in the cochlea is impeded. This can be caused by a build up of wax in the ear, or foreign objects in the outer ear canal. One of the most common forms of conductive loss is an excess of fluid in the middle ear and young children especially are prone to this condition (see Glue Ear on page 23).

Sensory loss: caused by damage to the nerves. There are no medical or surgical procedures that can help restore hearing if the loss is sensory. In many cases, hearing aids are prescribed to maximise residual hearing (hearing aids must be prescribed by an ENT specialist). A Cochlea Implant may be offered to a child whose hearing loss is too profound for hearing aids to help.

Mixed loss: a mixture of conductive and sensory loss, usually found in young children. The conductive element can be helped by medical and/or surgical procedures.

Degree of loss

Mild: the child hears nearly all speech, but may mishear if not looking directly at the speaker, or if acoustics in the classroom are poor. This condition can be very difficult to identify.

Moderate: the child will have great difficulty in hearing without a hearing aid anyone speaking who is not very close by. He or she may well rely on lipreading and visual cues to aid understanding, without realizing it. The child's own voice will give few clues to his or her having a hearing loss, but if you listen carefully, you may notice that he or she misses word endings such as ss, sh and leaves out indefinite and definite articles (e.g. the, a).

Severe: not able to cope without a hearing aid or even with one, the child needs to use visual clues such as lipreading and body language to gain information. The spoken voice may be comprehensible but the child is limited in the use of verbs and adjectives. Sentences may be shortened and sound somewhat 'telegraphic' in construction.

Profound: the child will probably use a hearing aid but will rely on visual cues and/or British Sign Language to communicate. The child's own voice may seem incomprehensible to those not used to it, but many youngsters achieve a high level of oral language. Radio aids are sometimes used with children who have severe or profound hearing loss. These use radio waves to transmit the speaker's voice to the listener and consists of two parts: a transmitter worn by the speaker (teacher) and a receiver worn by the child.

The majority of children with a hearing impairment in mainstream schools will have mild to moderate hearing loss and use oral/aural methods as their main mode of communication.

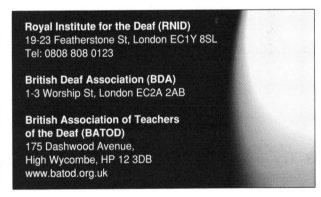

Royal Institute for the Deaf (RNID)
19-23 Featherstone St, London EC1Y 8SL
Tel: 0808 808 0123

British Deaf Association (BDA)
1-3 Worship St, London EC2A 2AB

British Association of Teachers of the Deaf (BATOD)
175 Dashwood Avenue,
High Wycombe, HP 12 3DB
www.batod.org.uk

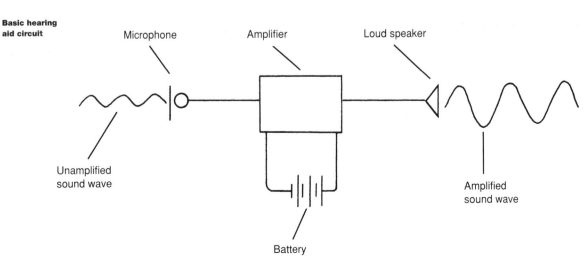

Basic hearing aid circuit

Microphone — Amplifier — Loud speaker

Unamplified sound wave

Battery

Amplified sound wave

INDIVIDUAL EDUCATION PLAN

Name:	**Area of concern:** Language impairment
Year: 2	**Strengths:** Drawing
Stage:	**Teacher/Support:** 5 hours LSA
Start date:	
Review date:	
IEP no.:	

Targets:

1. To be able to answer 'when' and 'who' questions.
2. To use 'word trees' to learn new vocabulary for the geography work.
3. To play ALS games in a group of 5/6.
4. To read two individual readers per week.

Strategies for use in class:

1. Ask another pupil a question first and then ask the same question of x to check understanding.
2. Ask x to repeat what she thinks she has to do for a task to check understandings.
3. Use x's ability to draw as an alternate form of recording.
4. Use some LSA time for individual reading sessions.
5. Present instructions in pictorial form if there are several.
6. Liaise with parents over the speech and language programme.
7. Make use of writing frames to aid writing.

Role of Parent(s)/Carer(s):

1. To liaise with school regularly over language programme.
2. To hear x read at least 3 times per week.
3. To play games provided.

Success criteria:

1. Being able to answer 'when/who' questions about a variety of texts and in different lessons.
2. To be able to reproduce word trees for at least 6 new words from the geography work.
3. Playing the ALS games observing the conventions of playing a game with a group, i.e. turn taking, talking, etc.
4. Evidence in the reading diary – this should include evidence of discussion work.

Resources:

1. Language programme provided by the Speech and Language Therapist.
2. Picture cards for discussion.
3. Instruction templates – to add pictures.
4. ALS games.
5. Five hours LSA time – one hour per day to include 20 minutes for language programme, 20 minutes individual reading sessions, 20 minutes ALS games with a group.
6. Writing frames.

Agreed by:

SENCO:

Parent(s)/Carer(s):

Pupil:

Date:

Language Impairment

Some children do not develop speech and language as expected. They may have difficulties with any or all aspects of speech and language, ranging from moving the muscles that control speech to the ability to understand or use language at all. The effects of language impairment can range from mild and transient to severe and long-term. It is estimated that six in 100 children will have speech, language or communication difficulties at some stage and that one in 500 will experience severe, long-term difficulties. Most classroom teachers will have a child with some difficulties in their class.

What are the causes?

There is a range of causes and it is important to remember that language difficulties affect different aspects of the language system and can result in different patterns of performance. Some of those causes include:

● Genetics – language impairment can be inherited
● The environment – there is a link between disadvantage and poor language skills
● Injury – this can include brain injury
● Illness – such as a stroke, Multiple Sclerosis or Motor Neurone Disease
● Hearing problems
● General learning difficulties
● A biological difficulty such as a cleft palate

What is language impairment?

There are different areas of language learning and, therefore, different forms of language impairment:

Speech apparatus – this includes the mouth, tongue, lips, nose, muscles and breathing. Any one, or all of these can be functioning incorrectly or inefficiently and lead to a language impairment. Some children will suffer from dysfluency or stammering.

Phonology – this refers to the sounds that make up the language. If a child has difficulty with phonology they use the wrong sounds.

Syntax or grammar – this is the way that words are put together in phrases or sentences. Some children cannot put the words together so that they can be understood.

Semantics – refers to the meaning of words and sentences. Children can find it difficult to remember the meaning of words.

Pragmatics – refers to how language is used in different situations and how feelings are conveyed.

Prosody (intonation and stress) – refers to the rhythm of the way we speak.

Within all of the above some children have difficulties with either receptive or expressive language, and some with both:

Receptive language – understanding the meaning of what others say.

Expressive language – using language to communicate so that others understand what you say.

Education and participation in society depend on the ability to communicate. Some children have specific language difficulties but others have additional difficulties such as hearing problems or motor difficulties.

Aphasia/dysphasia – these two terms are now accepted to mean the same and refer to a disorder of language. The ability to understand and express words is affected. In turn this can affect the understanding of speech, reading, speaking, writing, gesture and/or signing, using numbers or doing calculations. Those who suffer often explain this as knowing what they want to say but being unable to remember the words. Aphasia can be either acquired or developmental.

What is the impact of language impairment?

Language impairment can be isolating and distressing. It can lead to a loss of confidence, lack of self-esteem and affect personal and social relationships. Also, it reduces opportunities in education. Research indicates that children with more complex language problems have a greater likelihood of experiencing behaviour problems. It can also affect concentration and memory. Children with speech and language impairments need to be taught the speech, language and social communication skills that other children learn naturally. The best results are gained where there is early intervention.

How can we help?

● Speech and language therapy – refer as soon as possible.
● Regular speech and language sessions with either a teacher or trained assistant following a programme from the therapist.
● Use signs and gestures.
● Use pictures and/or symbols (as teaching aids or as prompt cards).
● Speak in short, simple sentences.
● Give one instruction at a time.
● Give a written list of instructions if appropriate.
● Ask the children to repeat what they think they have to do, to check understanding.
● Use circle time and social stories.
● Teach word association skills for word-finding difficulties.
● Use games to encourage listening and social skills.
● Have a 'word of the day/week' for the whole class.
● Use individual reading sessions to talk about pictures, storylines or meanings as appropriate to the age of the child.
● Teach the meanings of jokes, puns, etc.
● Be aware that misunderstanding can lead to possible behaviour and/or social problems.

ICAN
4 Dyer's Buildings, Holborn, London EC1N 2QP
Tel: 0870 225 4072
www.afasic.org.uk
www.ican.org.uk
www.ukconnect.org
www.cafamily.org.uk

INDIVIDUAL EDUCATION PLAN

Name:	**Area of concern:** Handwriting (left handed)
Year: 2	**Strengths:** Keen to do well
Stage:	**Teacher/Support:**
Start date:	
Review date:	
IEP no.: 2	

Targets:

1. To sit correctly at the table with paper tilted to the right.
2. To be able to use a pair of scissors to cut out accurately.
3. To form letters so that descenders are clear.

Strategies for use in class:

1. Make sure x is not sitting to the right of a right-handed child.
2. Encourage the use of Berol writing pen for ease of flow.
3. Encourage good posture at the table with feet on the floor.
4. Mark paper/book position on the table with tape until correct position established.
5. Ensure left-handed scissors are kept separately and clearly marked.
6. Have lots of practice work for letter formation.

Role of Parent(s)/Carer(s):

1. To encourage letter formation write in air, on margarine carton lids, etc.
2. To play cutting out, making models, etc.

Success criteria:

1. Demonstrating correct sitting position without being reminded.
2. The ability to cut out a variety of shapes accurately.
3. Letters written consistently in prose with clear descenders.

Resources:

1. Berol pens.
2. Brightly coloured masking tape to anchor/position paper.
3. Left-handed scissors.
4. 'One-a-day' practice sheets, Teodorescu writing books.

Agreed by:

SENCO:

Parent(s)/Carer(s):

Pupil:

Date:

Left-handed Writers

I t is estimated that around ten per cent of children are left-handed. There are different levels of left-side-preference; one pupil may write and draw with his left hand, kick a football with his left foot and also be left-eye dominant, while another may be left-handed but right-footed and right-eye dominant. Such a pupil may be described as cross-lateral and may be clumsy due to his left eye and right hand not co-ordinating very well.

Parents and teachers used to discourage children from using their left hand – to the extent of tying it behind their back, or making them sit on their left hand during lessons. Nowadays it is considered more sensible to allow children to develop right or left hand dominance naturally and to do all that we can to alleviate any problems caused by being left-handed in a mainly right-handed world.

In school, the activity likely to cause the most concern to left-handed children is writing. If you are right-handed, take a few minutes to transfer your pen to the left hand and write a few sentences; you will find that it is much harder to push the pen across the page than it is to pull it, you can't easily see what you have written and your normal (undoubtedly correct) letter formation becomes much more tricky. There are ways, however, of making life in the classroom easier for left-handers.

How can we help?

Position
- Avoid the situation where a left-handed child has a right-handed child next to him or her on her left: both youngsters will be competing for the same elbow room.
- Ensure a good writing posture; this calls for furniture of the correct size so that the child can put both feet on the floor and place his or her arms comfortably on the table. It can help left-handed writers to raise their seat slightly, giving a better view of their writing. A sloping surface sometimes helps too.
- The position of the paper can make a big difference to ease of writing; tilt to the right for a left-handed writer.

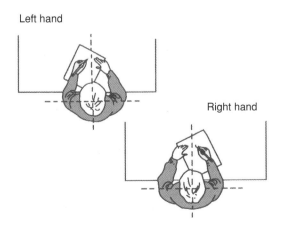
Left hand

Right hand

Modelling writing
Demonstrate letter formation with your left hand for left-handed writers.

Pencil grip
Children develop all sorts of penholds, though one of the best ways to hold a pencil, allowing for easy, controlled movement, is the tripod grip. The most important consideration is that the penhold is relaxed and comfortable; there is no right or wrong way and once a penhold is established, it is very difficult to change. If the child grips too tightly, presses very hard on the paper or twists his or her hand awkwardly, the act of writing can become very uncomfortable and difficult to sustain.

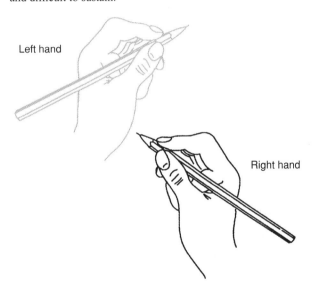
Left hand

Right hand

Materials
- The choice of paper and pen/pencil can make a huge difference. Try writing neatly with a stub of wax crayon on sugar paper! There is a huge range of pens and pencils from which to choose and it is worth encouraging a left-handed child, in particular, to experiment.
- For those who have difficulty in holding a writing implement comfortably, various types of grip are available which can be attached to the pen or pencil and may be of help.
(Remember to provide left-handed scissors for cutting out.)

Practice
A left-handed writer may need to practise more in the early stages; put together a selection of handwriting activities which he or she can practice at home and explain to parents or carers how they can help and encourage.

Left 'n Write
5 Charles St, Worcester WR1 2AQ
Tel: 01905 25798
www.lefthand-education.co.uk

INDIVIDUAL EDUCATION PLAN

Name:

Year: 7

Stage:

Area of concern: Literacy difficulties

Strengths: Enjoys reading and having books read to him

Teacher/Support: LSA to support in English lessons

Start date:

Review date:

IEP no.:

Targets:

1. To answer questions about a text:
   a. verbally
   b. in multiple choice exercises
   c. in short written sentences.
2. To practise reading every day and complete three books from the 'blue box' every week.
3. To improve spelling accuracy.
4. To write legibly and more quickly.

Strategies for use in class:

1. Give x frequent opportunities to follow text as you read out loud.
2. Check his understanding by questioning.
3. Encourage him to use his key word dictionary and provide a word wall of subject-specific vocabulary. Use the Look-Cover-Write-Check method for learning spellings.
4. Give praise for correct spellings.
5. Specify how much writing x should complete in a lesson (it requires a huge effort for him to write 50 words which are legible) and insist that it is legible.
6. Provide a pen if he has lost/forgotten his own.
7. Make use of alternative methods of recording where appropriate: diagram, poster, audio recording, word processing.

Role of Parent(s)/Carer(s):

1. Regular reading; Monday, Monday, Wednesday, Thursday after tea for fifteen minutes – X reading to you, or you reading to him. Talk about the stories, 'Which bit did you like best? What would you do if . . .?'
2. Writing the shopping list on Friday night – help him out with spellings.

Success criteria:

1. To complete the first three units of work in the scheme, with 80% accuracy.
2. To read three books each week with Mrs z, during the lunchtime study session.
3. To spell 100 key words correctly.
4. To finish pieces of writing in subject lessons and in a legible hand.

Resources:

1. Student books from the scheme.
2. Reading books from the blue box (reading age 7–8).
3. 'Talking books' on loan to take home.
4. Handwriting practice sheets.
5. Key words dictionary and LCWC book.

Agreed by:

SENCO:

Parent(s)/Carer(s):

Pupil:

Date:

Moderate Learning Difficulties (MLD)

The largest group of children and young adults with special educational needs are those defined as having Moderate Learning Difficulties (MLD), or Global Learning Difficulties (GLD). These are pupils with general developmental delay. They are increasingly placed in mainstream schools and may constitute as much as 20 per cent of any school population. They may once have been referred to as 'slow learners' or 'remedials' and, for the most part, will be found in the 'bottom sets' in school. These pupils do not find learning easy and often experience very little success in school. Their self-esteem can plummet, especially in secondary school and this may result in unacceptable behaviour as they search for a way of avoiding failure, putting on a show of bravado and impressing their peers.

The main characteristics

- Difficulties with reading and writing, and comprehension
- Poor understanding of basic mathematical concepts
- Immature social and emotional skills
- Limited communication skills
- Short attention span
- Underdeveloped co-ordination skills
- Lack of logical reasoning
- Inability to generalize what they learn and apply it to other situations

They may have problems with:

- Understanding what is required of them
- Remembering what has been taught (short-term and long-term)
- Acquiring sequencing skills
- Dyspraxia ('clumsiness')
- Organizing themselves
- Auditory/visual memory.

They may also have a variety of syndromes and/or medical conditions.

How can we help?

Children with moderate learning difficulties are often very conscious that they are 'lagging behind'. Everything possible should be done to enhance their self-esteem and persuade them that they can learn, albeit with a great deal of effort.

- Find out as much about the child as possible. Use SAT scores, reading age and any diagnostic data, to help you ascertain strengths and weaknesses.
- Use your own observation skills to build up a profile of the child, noticing how he or she responds to different teaching styles.
- Make sure that the learning objectives are realistic for every lesson, and that the child can experience some success.

- Break down any new task into small steps and build in lots of opportunities for reinforcement.
- Be prepared to allow the child extra time to finish a task.
- Check understanding at every stage.
- Establish a supportive relationship.
- Use appropriate praise and encouragement: catch the child being good as well as complimenting him or her for finishing work and trying hard.
- Liaise with the SENCO who will be able to suggest strategies and resources: differentiated texts, word banks, language master, writing frames, ICT software (and modified hardware).

It may be necessary to prepare individual work sometimes for a pupil or a small group; enlarging the print and shortening a passage is a simple process which can make an immediate difference to the accessibility of text. Make an overhead transparency of the text and project this while you read it out, perhaps several times, then let pupils practise together before having a go on their own. Children who struggle with reading need to have frequent practice in every subject of the curriculum. Provide writing frames or activity sheets which minimize the amount of writing required; if the child is involved in a science experiment, you want him to observe and record what happens, not spend 40 minutes trying to draw a bunsen burner.

- Establish a routine within the lesson so that pupils know what to expect and, most importantly, what is expected of them.
- Keep tasks short and build in variety.
- Establish what the child already knows about a topic; be prepared to go back to the point where he or she is on firm ground.
- Repeat information in different ways.
- Use careful questioning to ensure the child's participation and check his or her understanding.
- Short, daily practice of key skills like telling the time, multiplication tables and spellings is more effective than longer sessions.
- Show the child what to do as well as talking about it: give concrete examples, provide a model.

Learning assistants

Learning assistants can be an invaluable asset to teachers. The objectives of the lesson, and any differentiation required for MLD pupils to achieve, should be discussed between teacher and LSA so that there is adequate preparation and a shared understanding of goals. Sometimes, pupils can come to depend on their LSA for propping them up. It is important to encourage independence and establish a relationship which is supportive without being cosseting.

INDIVIDUAL EDUCATION PLAN

Name:

Year:

Stage:

Start date:

Review date:

IEP no.: 3

Area of concern: Visual impairment – requires modified resources (min. 14pt text). Reluctant to accept support. Monoaural

Strengths: Able and determined

Teacher/Support: TA. Sensory Inclusion Service

Targets:	Strategies for use in class:	Success criteria:	Resources:	Role of Parent(s)/Carer(s):
1. To complete appropriate tasks each day with adult support.	1. Set achievable tasks in discussion with VI teacher. Reward chart. Display completed work.	1. The required number of tasks completed on a daily basis – begin with one per day and increase with success.	1. Reward chart and stickers. Timer. Strategies from VI teacher.	1. Regular liaison through school diary.
2. To raise her hand for attention rather than calling out.	2. To sit at the front, facing the teacher. Ensure good right ear is to the teacher. General reminder to everyone. Ignore unwanted behaviour, positive acknowledgement of appropriate behaviour.	2. Achieved on 8 out of 10 occasions over the week's lessons.	2. Prompt card on desk. Prompt poster by the side of whiteboard. Rules of conduct up in every room. Appropriate room layout to maximize hearing.	2. Praise for completed tasks recorded in diary – set one task to be done at home each evening.
3. To try to form letters correctly, ensuring uniform size and inclination.	3. Use of appropriate handwriting equipment, resources. Praise success. Use of guidelines under paper.	3. Letters of uniform size, neatly on the line and sloping the same way in at least three separate pieces of work over the week.	3. Tripod grip pens with enlarged shaft to aid grip. Lined sheet to go under page. Opportunities to practise other than during lessons – including at home. Nelson/Ginn Handwriting books.	3. Use practical opportunities for handwriting, e.g. shopping lists.

Agreed by:

SENCO:

Parent(s)/Carer(s):

Pupil:

Date:

Multi-Sensory Impairment

Children and young people who have a combination of both visual and hearing difficulties may be described as having multi-sensory impairment. This is often referred to as deafblindness, but it is important to remember that an individual may have some residual hearing or sight. Many of these children and young people will also have additional problems but it can be difficult to work out the extent of any cognitive difficulties because of the complexities of their deafblindness.

When a child is born with a combination of sight and hearing difficulties this is known as **congenital deafblindness**.

When a young person develops these problems later this is known as **acquired deafblindness**.

In the UK there are about 23,000 people who are deafblind. It is only recently that there has been a better understanding of the deafblind population and how it is changing. In the first half of the twentieth century hundreds of babies were born with congenital rubella syndrome (CRS) where heart, sight and hearing were affected. Since 1970, however, the numbers of children affected by rubella have fallen dramatically because of vaccination campaigns, so that between 1991 and 1996 fewer than 33 babies were born with CRS.

Congenital rubella syndrome is therefore no longer the most common cause of deafblindness and the reasons for the continuing difficulties of multi-sensory impairment are complex. A recent survey showed that there were many causes for deafblindness including:

- premature birth
- birth trauma and/or asphyxia
- viral infections
- chromosome abnormalities.

Usher Syndrome

Usher Syndrome is a genetic condition where a baby is born deaf or with partial hearing and loses his or her sight during the teenage years. Since 1983 information about the condition has developed enormously and three types of Usher Syndrome have been identified:

1. Children with **Usher 1** are born profoundly deaf and usually grow up as part of the deaf community. They generally start to lose their sight in their teens, with tunnel vision and night blindness being the first signs.
2. Children with **Usher 2** are born with partial hearing and often wear hearing aids. They are most likely to have grown up as part of the 'hearing' community. As with Usher 1 sight begins to be lost during the teenage years.
3. People with **Usher 3** are born with normal hearing but develop problems with both sight and hearing later in life.

Ninety-five per cent of what we learn about ourselves and the world comes through the dominant senses of sight and hearing, and therefore those children and young people who are deafblind face tremendous challenges, especially in learning to communicate and accessing the curriculum. As deafblind children develop in very different ways, the challenges that each faces will be very different. A young person who is blind and also has a hearing loss must be treated in a different way to a young person who is blind but has good hearing: their needs are very different. Improved diagnosis and awareness mean that provision to meet the needs of individuals can now be arranged more effectively.

Teaching approaches need to make good use of any residual sight or hearing an individual may have, together with their other senses. Strategies need to make the most of tactile learning opportunities and alternative means of communication. Alternative modes of communication include:

- Braille
- British Sign Language (BSL)
- Makaton
- Objects of Reference
- Total Communication
- Deaf-Blind manual alphabet

(See also the section on Augmented and Alternative Communication.)

How can we help?

- Talk to parents/carers; share information in partnership.
- Discuss communication needs with the young person (where appropriate).
- Use multi-sensory resources – especially tactile ones.
- Develop a buddy system.
- Ensure appropriate placement in a classroom that makes the most of any residual sight or hearing.
- Ensure that classrooms, school corridors, etc. are arranged for ease of movement.
- Make use of the many programmes that have been developed for use with ICT.
- Assess for any augmented and alternative communication aids.
- Make use of specialist advice available from, for example, Sensory Services or Speech and Language Therapists.

Royal National Institute of the Blind (RNIB)
www.rnib.org.uk
Royal National Institute for the Deaf (RNID)
www.rnid.org.uk
SENSE
www.sense.org.uk

INDIVIDUAL EDUCATION PLAN

Name:

Year:

Stage:

Area of concern: Semantic Pragmatic Disorder

Strengths: Rote memory

Teacher/Support:

Start date:

Review date:

IEP no.: 2

Targets:

1. To use a task board each session.
2. To be able to take part in a game with two other children.
3. To organize the lunch boxes.
4. To learn to put a hand up and wait for help when needed.

Strategies for use in class:

1. Make instructions explicit.
2. Prepare for any changes to routine.
3. Ask him to repeat what he has to do to check for meaning.
4. Model how to organize lunch boxes, including how to talk to people.
5. Use cards to reinforce the hands up rule.
6. During literacy and numeracy ask straightforward questions and allow time to answer.
7. Build in work on explaining jokes.
8. Make good use of computer programs.

Role of Parent(s)/Carer(s):

1. Regular contact with class teacher.
2. To play literacy and numeracy games at home.
3. To share stories.

Success criteria:

1. Being able to follow the task board without help.
2. Taking part on at least five different occasions.
3. Showing that he has learnt the appropriate language and can organize appropriately.
4. No longer getting out of seat to fetch an adult.

Resources:

1. Task board and stickers.
2. LSA for five hours per week – to include 10 minutes per day on language work.
3. Literacy and numeracy games – from ALS pack.
4. Resources provided by Speech and Language Therapist.
5. Circle time/social stories resources.

Agreed by:

SENCO:

Parent(s)/Carer(s):

Pupil:

Date:

Semantic Pragmatic Disorder (SPD)

Semantic Pragmatic Disorder is a communication disorder (semantic refers to the meanings of words and sentences, while pragmatic means making language work in context). Children with SPD have difficulty in processing all the information from a situation and often do not respond appropriately.

The disorder relates to autism in that it involves difficulties in the same three areas: socializing, language and imagination ('The Triad').

Switched off

Most children absorb information easily, processing and analysing it, discarding what is unimportant or uninteresting and storing the rest. They are able to build up a memory bank of words and their meanings, including those which relate to concepts such as time and personal feelings, which may not have a visual reference. They use this data, together with their past experience of the world, to predict how other people will react to certain things, to understand their intentions and forecast what might happen next.

A child with SPD has an imperfect 'information processing' system and will have problems in knowing what to say, sometimes appearing rude or outspoken, and not realizing that the listener has 'had enough'. He may talk at great length about something which interests him, but not realize that the listener has 'switched off'.

The main characteristics

- speaks fluently, sometimes in a very grown-up way, but on his or her own terms
- uses inappropriate eye-contact/facial expression
- has difficulty in giving specific information
- has problems with abstract concepts (imagine, guess, next week)
- can appear rude, arrogant, gauche
- is easily distracted
- has motor skills problems
- is over-sensitive to certain noises, etc.

In school, these children need:

- straightforward, specific and unambiguous instructions, e.g. 'put the pencils in the blue box', not 'tidy up'
- practical, hands-on tasks
- a quiet, orderly working environment
- predictability in the classroom routine – give clear signals for any changes
- time to reply when asked a question
- specific activities to help with socializing
- clear rules on how to behave
- regular reminders, supported by visual/written information (e.g. a task board)
- adults to interpret what the child 'means' rather than accept what he or she actually says when it doesn't make sense
- explanations about sarcasm, metaphors, jokes – do not take for granted that they understand
- a teacher to double-check their understanding
- to be taught the meanings of idiomatic expressions and appropriate language for different situations
- constant encouragement and praise.

National Autistic Society
www.nas.org.uk
email: nas@mailbox.ulcc.ac.uk

INDIVIDUAL EDUCATION PLAN

Name:

Year: 6

Stage:

Area of concern: Tourette's Syndrome

Strengths: ICT skills

Teacher/Support: 5 hours SSA

Start date:

Review date:

IEP no.:

Targets:

1. To be able to remove self from room when necessary.
2. To attend computer club at lunch times (to relieve stress of unstructured times).
3. To walk away and report any incidents of teasing (rather than retaliation).

Strategies for use in class:

1. A small card that will be displayed on the table to indicate a need to leave.
2. Encouraging reminders to the whole class of times for computer club.
3. x has agreed that Tourette's Syndrome can be used as a discussion for PSHE alongside other conditions.
4. Allow x to sit at the back of the class where he feels comfortable.
5. If you notice the tics becoming more regular use the card to indicate time out is needed.
6. Make regular use of the computer to aid written tasks and concentration.
7. Encourage peer mentoring.

Role of Parent(s)/Carer(s):

1. To keep staff informed.
2. To help with homework

Success criteria:

1. Having demonstrated the ability to do this appropriately on five separate occasions.
2. Attendance on a regular basis of twice a week as agreed.
3. No incidences of fights because of teasing.

Resources:

1. A copy of x's indication card will be available in the teacher's desk in all rooms.
2. Further information on Tourette's Syndrome available in the staff room in *Special Children* folder.
3. A space has been made available in the library for use if needed.
4. A separate room has been organized for x to take his SATs.
5. Parents have provided a full description of how TS affects x and the signs to look for.

Agreed by:

SENCO:

Parent(s)/Carer(s):

Pupil:

Date:

Tourette's Syndrome

Tourette's Syndrome is one of a number of tic disorders. It is characterised by many varied, frequently changing tics. Current research indicates that it is an inability to regulate dopamine (a neuro-transmitter) resulting in the impaired action of various receptor sites. It is a neurobiological disorder that is genetically inherited. It can be triggered by a streptococcal infection: however, it is not the infection itself that causes the trigger but the body's antibodies. It is estimated that three per cent of the population may have Tourette's Syndrome with a ratio of four to one males to females.

What is a tic?

A tic is an involuntary rapid or sudden movement or sound that is repeated over and over again. A tic can start as blinking or sniffing or can progress to be as extreme as coprolalia, copropraxia, echolalia or echopraxia.

Coprolalia – the repetition of obscene words.
Copropraxia – the repetition of obscene gestures.
Echolalia – the repetition of what you last heard.
Echopraxia – imitating the actions you saw.

It must be stressed that the majority of children have Tourette's Syndrome in the mild form and are probably undiagnosed. The extreme forms mentioned above are only found in a minority but tend to hit the headlines!

Tics often disappear during sleep (though not always). They are usually worse during times of stress and/or excitement and when the child is extremely tired. It is interesting for schools to note that they can subside during periods of extreme concentration such as at a computer or when engaged in a favourite activity.

People who suffer from tics say that they are often aware when they are going to occur, but that it is like a sneeze in that they can do nothing about it. Some people learn to suppress their tics for a while but that will mean they return with a vengeance once the person relaxes.

Transient tics – one in five children will have a tic at some time but these are mainly transient and only last a few weeks or months. They may have several episodes over several years and they may change from one to another, such as from sniffing to hair twirling.

Chronic tic disorder – this is where the tics do not change and will remain unchanged for years. A person may have several chronic tics.

Treatment

This is often not necessary and an explanation may be all that is needed to help the individual understand. If the tics are causing problems then medication can be prescribed but there is a period of trial before identifying which provides the optimum benefit.

Types of Tourette's Syndrome:

1. Pure Tourette's Syndrome – often goes undiagnosed and is not associated with other conditions.
2. Full blown Tourette's Syndrome – include the extremes such as coprolalia and/or copropraxia.

3. Tourette's Syndrome Plus – associated conditions are present.

Pure Tourette's Syndrome often causes no behavioural or educational problems but it is the associated disorders that lead to difficulties:

- Attention Deficit Hyperactivity Disorder (ADHD)
- Obsessive Compulsive Disorder (OCD)
- Oppositional Defiant Disorder (ODD)
- Self-injurious behaviour
- Outbursts of aggression
- Depression
- Fine motor control problems
- Organizational problems
- Reading comprehension difficulties.

Children with Tourette's Syndrome follow the normal curve of distribution of intelligence: however, they are more likely to experience learning difficulties than the general population. The condition is often misunderstood and everyone associated with the child needs a knowledge and understanding of how it affects the individual child.

How can we help?

- Talk to the parents (and child if appropriate).
- Prevent teasing at all costs.
- Allow extra time to prevent stress.
- Provide time-out for when tics become disruptive.
- Have a discrete sign so that the individual can leave to release tics in private.
- Encourage students to monitor themselves so they know when they need a break.
- Allow the child to sit at the back to prevent staring.
- Provide a separate room for exams.
- Be flexible – if reading is affected by eye/neck tics, then provide an alternative.
- If the child has loud vocal tics, allow him or her to miss large group, quiet times such as assembly.
- Make use of a computer to cut down on handwriting.
- Use multi-sensory strategies, especially practical activities.
- Pair with a mentor if the tics would make an activity unsafe, such as an experiment.
- If it is a touching tic allow for a buffer zone (but be careful not to isolate the child).
- Plan for times of excitement such as birthdays, trips, etc.
- A library carrel or private area may help.
- If tics are exhausting, break work into smaller chunks.
- Be watchful of depression.
- Do NOT punish a tic!

Tourette's Syndrome (UK) Association
PO Box 26149
Dunfermline
KY12 9WT
www.tsa.org.uk

Safety Considerations

- Use textured flooring where possible to differentiate between areas.

- Floor coverings should be checked regularly for holes: check for slippery surfaces and crumbling steps outside.

- Paint white strips on steps, stairs and hand rails.

- Stick transfers or pictures on large expanses of plain glass.

- Keep classroom floors free of clutter such as schoolbags, coats and electric cables; make sure that corridors are 'clearways'.

- Avoid having objects hanging at head height – plants, mobiles, 'washing lines for paintings', or make sure the child knows exactly where the 'obstacles' are.

- Beware of windows at head height which open out into a thoroughfare, or on to the playground.

- Have good, consistent lighting around the school.

- Make sure that other pupils understand how they can help the child with visual impairment, e.g. by refraining from swinging backwards on their chairs, or suddenly pushing back their chair to get up.

- Encourage orderly movement around the school, a 'keep to the left' system and no running.

- Teach pupils to take special care with sharp objects such as scissors.

Visual Impairment

The vast majority of children with sight problems are educated in mainstream schools where, given appropriate support, they can thrive. In some cases however, children's problems are not recognized or sufficiently understood and it is in these cases that problems tend to arise.

Teachers and learning assistants are well placed to observe children carefully and take note of any behaviour which indicates a sight problem; further investigation by a GP or optician should always be recommended to parents and carers where there is concern.

The main characteristics

- Inflamed, weepy, cloudy or bloodshot eyes
- Squints and eyes that do not seem to be aligned and working together
- Rapid, involuntary eye movements
- Continual blinking, rubbing or screwing-up of eyes
- Discomfort in bright light
- The child holding his or her head in an awkward position or holding a book at an unusual angle/distance
- Frequent headaches or dizziness
- Clumsiness, bumping into furniture, etc.
- Poor balance
- Failure to respond appropriately to questions, commands or gestures unless addressed directly by name; inappropriate response to nonverbal communication
- Difficulty in copying from the board, poor presentation skills, confusion between similarly shaped letters/words

Symptoms such as these may result in the child being unable to engage with the learning task in hand and so becoming 'switched off'.

How can we help?

- If the child has glasses, encourage him or her to wear them and to keep them clean.
- Find out from the specialist visual impairment teacher as much as you can about the child's condition and the implications for classroom work.
- Always give clear instructions and descriptions – the child may misread gestures and facial expressions.
- Use the child's name to get attention – looking at him or her may not be enough.
- Allow the child to sit at the front of the class or near to the board, big book, television or overhead projector screen. Provide his or her own copy of the text where possible.

- Allow extra time for finishing tasks.
- Always provide the child with a book of his or her own rather than expecting the child to share.
- Do not stand with your back to the window; this creates silhouetting and makes it harder for the child to see you.
- Make sure that there is good lighting in work areas, with no glare. Some children are photophobic (sensitive to light), and may be more comfortable in a shaded area of the room.
- The pupil with impaired vision will tire more quickly than his or her peers – short tasks are preferable to long, sustained sessions.
- Draw the child's attention to displays – otherwise they may go unnoticed.
- Encourage personal tidiness and identify some personal space for the visually impaired child. Pegs and lockers should be at the end of rows and not shared
- Find out about specialist equipment that can enable the child to be more independent in practical lessons (e.g. talking scales).

All resource material should be of good quality and well spaced:

- Avoid cluttering the pages of worksheets with illustrations and ornate script.
- Enlarge the text to

16 point or 18 point

where possible.
- Avoid *italic* or *ornate* scripts.
- Remember that lower case script is easier to read than CAPITAL LETTERS, because it has ascenders and descenders to give it a more distinctive shape.
- Shorter lines of text are easier to follow, and an unjustified right hand margin helps the reader.
- Use paper with a matt surface rather than a glossy surface which may create glare.

The child with more severely impaired vision may need specialized equipment and there is a range of magnifying equipment which your visual impairment service will be able to advise on.

RNIB (Royal National institute for the Blind)
224 Great Portland Street,
London W1W 5AA
Tel: 020 7388 1266
www.rnib.org.uk

Asthma

An ever-increasing number of children are affected by asthma. Some experts say as many as one in seven children in the UK are affected by asthma, wheeze or chronic cough. The causes of this increase are not entirely clear. Exposure to traffic-related pollution has popularly been blamed as a major cause, and it is clear that asthma sufferers are more likely to experience an attack on polluted days. There is no firm evidence, however, to show that people who live in more polluted areas are necessarily more prone to be asthma sufferers in the first place. A wide range of other factors is also important. Exposure to tobacco smoke and house dust mite are certainly amongst the most serious risk factors; others include the presence of damp and mould, food additives, pollen and spores, and fur and feathers. Whatever the causes, asthma can be both a discomforting and a debilitating disease.

What is asthma?

Asthma is a common disease in which the circular smooth muscles of the branching air tubes of the lungs, the bronchi, are liable to go into spasm so that the bronchi are narrowed and the passage of air impeded. It is often easier to breathe in than out and the lungs become inflated and cannot easily be emptied. A wheeze on breathing out is a regular feature of an asthma attack. The commonest kind is allergic asthma, but asthma can also be induced by infection, emotion, occupation and exertion.

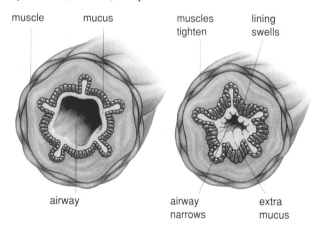

muscle   mucus   muscles   lining
                          tighten   swells

airway   airway   extra
                    narrows   mucus

Narrowing of the tubes carrying air into lungs, as a result of tightening of the muscles in their walls, is called 'bronchospasm'. While bronchospasm is the main feature of asthma, it also occurs in other allergic conditions and other lung diseases, such as emphysema and chronic bronchitis. The result of bronchospasm is a restriction in the flow of air. This is often worse on breathing out than breathing in and there may be severe wheezing and a persistently inflated chest. It also causes coughing. Sometimes bronchospasm is so severe as to endanger life. Commonly it leads to an inadequate supply of oxygen to the tissues, and the skin may appear blue (cyanosis).

An asthma attack can last for a few minutes or several hours, but sufferers learn to recognize the signs of the condition worsening and what to do to alleviate it. Asthma is treated with two main types of medicine, called relievers and preventers. Each medicine works in a different way, but both need to be breathed in deeply to reach the lungs. They come in small packs called inhalers or puffers.

Reliever medicines relieve the symptoms of asthma straight away by relaxing the muscles around the airways so that they open wider and make breathing easier. The medicine does not treat the inflammation in the airway itself. Reliever inhalers are usually blue and children must have access to their inhaler at all times.

Preventer medicines calm the inflamed airways and stop them being irritated so easily. This helps to calm the asthma and reduces the risk of an attack. The effect of the medicine builds up over time so it has to be taken every day.

How can we help?

There are no learning difficulties associated with asthma and all but the most severely affected children are able to cope in mainstream schools. It is important however that all staff know when a child has the condition and are familiar with the procedure to be followed if he has an attack. There are five basic rules:

- Stay calm – anxiety can aggravate the attack. Reassure the child, but don't put your arm round him or her.
- Find the child's reliever inhaler and make sure he or she uses it correctly.
- Encourage the child to sit upright and lean forwards.
- Loosen tight clothing and offer a drink of water.
- Call medical help if the medication fails to relieve the attack in five to ten minutes – the child should continue to use his or her reliever inhaler every few minutes until the doctor or ambulance arrives.

Asthma attacks are often brought on by exercise, especially in cold, dry weather; this can often be prevented by the use of an inhaler before a PE lesson and by 'warming-up' gradually. Care should be taken to ensure that a child does not use his asthma as an excuse to avoid PE. Regular exercise, especially swimming, is beneficial. Always check with parents or carers for guidance on this matter.

Asthma UK
Summit House
70 Wilson Street
London EC2A 2DB
Tel: 020 7786 5000
Advice line 08457 010203

Brittle Bones

Brittle Bones is a genetic disorder known medically as Osteogenesis Imperfecta (OI). Brittle Bones actually refers to a range of conditions resulting from abnormalities in the protein structure of the bones that leads to the bones breaking more easily. It is not caused by a lack of calcium. The milder forms are usually inherited but for others the genetic mutation happens 'out of the blue'. Because the genetic defect is dominant, a carrier has a 50 per cent chance of passing on the condition to his or her children. About one in 20,000 babies are born with Brittle Bones each year. There is no cure at present but work on treatment is progressing.

Some children are born with fractures; some suffer them soon after birth and others when they first start to walk. Children can suffer anything from ten to 100 or more fractures during childhood. There is no general indication of how frequently a child will suffer from fractures and some are more vulnerable than others. Each fracture has to be managed individually as it occurs. Sometimes children go through a 'bad spell' when they have several breaks one after another, and then they can go years without one. There is evidence to show that adolescents do not fracture as frequently as younger children. Fractures can be caused by perfectly normal behaviour such as closing a door or turning over in bed, and whereas schools should make every effort to ensure the safety of the child it should not be held responsible for any breaks that occur at school.

The main characteristics

Some children are of normal stature and simply more fragile, whereas others who are more severely affected can be of short stature and unable to walk. Children with the severe type may have spent much of their early life lying on their back in plaster and may have missed out on a range of experiences. This in turn can affect confidence and learning. There may be problems with gross motor skills and children may take longer to learn to walk or sit. Often children have lax joints and loose muscles that lead to difficulties with fine motor skills. Children with Brittle Bones are often left-handed because they experience fewer breaks with that arm. They may hold their pen or pencil with an unconventional grip and find it difficult to write for long periods. Most, given the right support, can lead active lives but many may need to use sticks, crutches or wheelchairs for support and safety. PE and games are not generally recommended but swimming and non-weight bearing exercise are beneficial. More unusual characteristics include a triangular shaped face, progressive limb deformities, chronic bone pain and hearing difficulties. Those who are most severely affected often have respiratory problems because of under-developed lungs.

The vast majority of children are of normal intelligence and have no needs other than physical ones. However, it is important to bear in mind the emotional needs of children growing up with a condition that they feel may restrict their lives. There is a balance to be found between being overprotective and allowing the freedom to take risks. Education is important as, given the right opportunities, children with the condition can lead independent lives.

How can we help?

- Talk to parents and the child.
- Get the advice of an Occupational Therapist – they will be able to help on simple adaptations and/or specialist equipment that may need to be made at each stage of education.
- Make use of specially adapted keyboards or voice-activated packages for computers if finger movement is restricted.
- For handwriting problems consider:
  - A sloping desk
  - Different sizes/shapes of pen
  - Seating arrangements
  - Providing handouts/copies of notes
  - Dictaphone.
- Make sure everyone is aware and knows what to do in the event of a break.
- With permission from the child and his or her parents, inform the child's peers through PSHE.
- Be flexible with arrangements for the playground and movement in school – allowing the child to leave a couple of minutes before or after everyone else should suffice.
- Use a buddy system to help at times such as lunch.
- Expect high academic standards.
- Provide pastoral support – this is particularly important as the child gets older.
- Ensure effective liaison between school and hospital and/or home tuition when needed.
- Plan ahead for transfers.
- Plan for time missed because of breaks.
- Encourage participation in out-of-school activities – depending on the severity of the condition, a child may feel socially isolated.
- Use a small cue card for children to call for help – they are often reluctant to do so because they do not like to feel any more different than they are already.

It is important to try to treat a child with Brittle Bones as normally as possible to ensure a healthy emotional development that will lead to independence.

Brittle Bone Society
www.brittlebone.org
Tel: (01382) 20 4446
Email: bbs@brittlebone.org

Diabetes

Diabetes is a health condition that affects about 1.4 million people in the United Kingdom, and it is estimated that another one million have the condition but don't know. About one in every 700 school children has the condition and both sexes are equally affected. It is a common condition in which the amount of glucose (sugar) in the blood is too high because the body's method of converting that glucose into energy is not working (the hormone insulin made by the pancreas normally controls it). It is important to remember that treatment is effective.

Types of Diabetes

There are two main types of diabetes, and over three-quarters of those affected have Type 2.

● Type 1

This occurs when there is a severe lack of insulin because the cells in the pancreas have been destroyed. It usually appears in people under forty and often in childhood. Symptoms develop quickly and are obvious. These children are treated with insulin injections, which are vital to keep them alive, and through a carefully managed diet. Most children will have two injections a day, usually before breakfast and before an evening meal. However, a few may also need a lunchtime injection.

● Type 2

This is the type commonly found in the over-forties. It occurs when the pancreas cannot produce enough insulin for the needs of the body. Diet alone, diet and tablets or diet and injections, depending on the severity of need, can treat this type. It develops slowly and the symptoms are less severe. It often goes unnoticed because the symptoms are put down to getting older and overwork.

What are the symptoms?
- Increased thirst
- Going to the toilet a lot
- Extreme tiredness
- Weight loss
- Genital itching
- Blurred vision

Adverse reactions

If the blood sugar becomes too low a person may develop **hypoglycaemia** and can become unconscious.
If the blood sugar is too high they may develop **hyperglycaemia**. It is the first of these two that is more likely to occur in school.

The causes:
- A missed snack – timing of food is important and some children may need to eat in lessons
- Extra exercise – it is important to encourage regular exercise but all staff must be aware that excessive exercise could lead to an episode if diet is not controlled

- Too much insulin
- Extremes of weather

The symptoms:
It is really important that everyone who comes into contact with the child is aware of these symptoms!

- Hunger
- Sweating
- Drowsiness
- Pallor
- Glazed eyes
- Shaking
- Mood change – especially aggression
- Lack of concentration

NB The parents and the child themselves will be able to tell you about their symptoms.

How to treat:
Give fast-acting sugar to raise blood glucose levels:

- Lucozade or other sugary drink – NOT diet varieties
- Mini chocolate bar
- Fresh fruit juice
- Glucose tablets
- Jam/honey – if the child is too confused to help him or herself try rubbing jam or honey in the inside of the cheek.

ALWAYS try to keep something for an emergency in the teacher's desk and in the child's pocket.
When a child recovers from an episode he or she will need some slower-acting starchy food such as a sandwich. He or she may feel nauseous, tired and/or have a headache.

In the unlikely event that the child loses consciousness, put him or her into the recovery position and call an ambulance.

Points to remember

- Allow the child to visit the toilet regularly.
- A younger child may need help with the timing of food.
- You may have to allow the child to be first in the dinner queue.
- Adolescents may rebel against the strict regime and may need some counselling.
- All staff should know the symptoms to look for and how to react.
- Regular exercise helps cut down on serious health problems later.

Diabetes UK
www.diabetes.org.uk
Careline: 0845 120 2960 Monday–Friday (9–5)

Epilepsy

Epilepsy is the second most common neurological disorder (after migraine). It affects one in about every 130 people in the UK and 75 per cent of them will have their first seizure before the age of 20. Most teachers will have at least one child with epilepsy in their class at some time in their career.

What is epilepsy?

The cause of epilepsy is a temporary change in the way brain cells work. An upset in brain chemistry means messages get scrambled and that causes neurons to fire off faster than usual. This 'electrical storm' interferes with normal functioning and triggers a seizure. There are 40 different types of seizure caused by different chemical processes, sited in different areas of the brain.

Types of seizure

There are two main types of seizure; a *partial seizure* occurs when a specific part of the brain is affected and the nature of such fits depends upon the area of brain involved. The child will not pass out but consciousness will be affected. With a *generalized seizure* a large part of the brain is affected. Fits vary from major convulsive episodes, with jerking of limbs and unconsciousness, to momentary lapses of consciousness and fluttering eyelids.

However, two people who have the same type of seizure may have dramatically different experiences. They can vary from 'absence seizures' where the child may appear to be daydreaming to full 'tonic' seizures, sometimes referred to as 'grand-mal'.

Treatment

The standard treatment is to give drugs that regulate the chemical processes in the brain and allow most children the chance to lead a 'normal' life. All the drugs aim to prevent rather than treat seizures, which is why those affected must take the same dose every day. All the drugs can cause side effects and it is important to monitor and change the drugs being used until the one that best suits an individual is found. If a child is drowsy or over-active it is vital to tell parents as this may be a sign that the medication needs adjusting.

Possible side effects of the drugs include dizziness, headaches, nausea, tiredness, poor memory, slow reaction times and impaired motor control.

With adequate supervision there is no activity that needs to be barred but if a child has a history of frequent or unpredictable seizures it is probably wise to avoid climbing the wall bars! Swimming should be encouraged but make sure that a 'buddy' system is set up first.

What can trigger a seizure?

Most seizures strike completely out of the blue but certain factors can act as a trigger:

- Stress
- Patterns of light – many people believe that watching TV or playing video games can trigger a seizure. This is true in a few people who are photosensitive (sensitive to flickering light), though it is far less common than most people imagine. In fact, only about five per cent of people with epilepsy are affected in this way
- Lack of sleep – too many late nights can trigger seizures
- Illness – a high temperature (fever) can bring on seizures
- Hormones – for some girls, seizures may be linked to their menstrual cycle
- Food – some people with epilepsy claim that certain foods trigger seizures. Apart from some severe types of childhood epilepsy, however, there is no evidence to suggest that what you eat can bring on seizures. Skipping meals and a poor diet may be a factor

How to deal with a seizure

- Cushion the head with something soft.
- Do not put anything in the mouth or between the teeth.
- Do not give anything to drink until the seizure finishes.
- Loosen tight clothing around the neck.
- As soon as possible, or when movements subside, put the child in a semi-prone position to aid breathing.
- Wipe away saliva.
- Keep calm – reassure the child, especially in that confused period immediately following a seizure.
- If incontinence occurs, cover with a blanket.
- There is no need for an ambulance unless the seizure lasts for more than five minute, or the child has a series of seizures without, properly regaining consciousness between them.
- Provide a place to rest.
- Always inform parents when a seizure has occurred.

Some general hints

- Talk to parents.
- All staff in school must know what to do.
- Allow for catching up missed work.
- Be alert and prevent teasing. Explain to other children.
- Respond calmly – remember other children may be frightened.
- Be alert for the 'daydreamer' – 30 to 40 absences per day can have a devastating effect on education.
- Ensure that school records have full details of medication, type of seizure, etc. in case of an emergency.

(See checklist over page.)

British Epilepsy Association
www.epilepsy.org.uk
National Society for Epilepsy
www.epilepsynse.org.uk

Seizure Checklist

When a child has a seizure . . .

- Do not try to hold the child down or stop him or her moving about.

- Put something soft under his or her head and loosen collar and tie.

- Move any furniture or anything with sharp edges so that the child will not hurt him or herself.

- Do not try to put anything in the child's mouth or make him or her drink anything.

- Wait quietly with the child until he or she knows where they are and what has happened.

- Ask the child if he or she wants to have a rest before going back to lessons.

- Do not ring for an ambulance unless the child has hurt himself or the seizure lasts longer than a few minutes.

- Explain to classmates what has happened and how they can help.

- Help the child to catch up with any work missed in class.

- Let the parents know.

Friedreich's Ataxia

Ataxia is the loss of body movement. Early signs can include clumsiness or unsteadiness, but vision, hearing and speech can also be affected.

Ataxia can have many causes including alcoholism, brain tumours or Multiple Sclerosis. Research shows that Foetal Alcohol Syndrome currently affects one in 300 babies in the UK and is now the biggest cause of non-genetic disability. This suggests many more children with ataxia will be seen in schools in the future. However, ataxia can also be caused by genetics and there are several types of inherited ataxia, which may be early-onset and start in childhood or late-onset and start in adulthood.

Although rare, Friedreich's Ataxia is the most prevalent inherited ataxia and affects about one in every 50,000. It affects both males and females equally and is an early-onset ataxia with symptoms usually appearing any age between 5 and 15 years. On rare occasions the signs can appear either at an earlier or later stage. Friedreich's Ataxia is an autosomal recessive disease, which means the person inherits two affected genes, one from each parent. It is named after the physician who first identified it in the early 1860s. The condition is caused by degeneration of nerve tissue in the spinal cord and of nerves that serve areas such as the legs and arms.

There is no known cure but many of the symptoms can be alleviated. Most people with Friedreich's Ataxia die in early adulthood, especially where there is significant heart disease, which is the most common cause of death. However, some people have less severe symptoms and live much longer.

Progress of the disease

The first symptom is often difficulty in walking with a weakness in the legs and unsteadiness in standing. Mild scoliosis (curvature of the spine) develops, together with reduced feeling in fingers and toes. This can result in problems with writing and other tasks and the scoliosis can affect breathing. Over time muscles weaken and waste away. Speech may become slow and slurred and the child may tire easily. As the eye muscles weaken sight can also be affected.

The rate of progress of the disease differs from one person to the next but in general the person will be in a wheelchair within eight to ten years of the onset stages.

Associated conditions

Heart disease is the most common associated condition and symptoms can include chest pain, shortness of breath and palpitations. These conditions can be helped with medication.

Diabetes is also associated with Friedreich's Ataxia but most people will develop this late in the course of the disease, and the link between the two has not yet been established. The diabetes can be helped through diet and insulin if necessary.

About 20 per cent of those with Friedreich's Ataxia develop intolerance to carbohydrates, but this again can be helped by a dietician. Some may lose their hearing or sight.

How can we help?

- Talk to parents – and the child when appropriate.
- Plan ahead but do not presume the course of the disease.
- Liaise with physiotherapy and occupational therapy regularly.
- Liaise with Sensory Teams.
- Use a buddy system, especially for help with carrying bags, etc.
- Make use of ICT, especially predictive text, and later, Augmentative and Alternative Communication devices.
- Ensure appropriate seating is available.
- Check that the PE programme is appropriate.
- Provide a room for rest if fatigue becomes an issue.
- Establish a key worker as this will be particularly important if there are periods away from school.
- The school's Accessibility Plan should plan for disabled facilities where they do not already exist. Shower facilities with hoists may be needed at a later stage.
- Think about classroom layout – is it easy to get around?
- Make sure after-school clubs are accessible.
- Facilitate staff counselling.
- Ensure all staff are aware of the implications, and especially that they are aware of the parents' wishes – for example, parents may not want their child to be fully aware of the implications of the disease at a particular point in time.
- Ensure the school has a clear medical policy.

Ataxia UK
10 Winchester House, Kennington Park,
Cranmer Road, London SW9 6EJ
Tel: 0207 820 3900
www.ataxia.org.uk
www.atsociety.org.uk

Muscular Dystrophy (MD)

Muscular dystrophy is a general term used to describe a group of about 20 types of genetic disorders that involve muscle weakness. It is caused by a fault on a particular gene that leads to damaged muscle fibres. Duchenne's Muscular Dystrophy is the most common childhood dystrophy and affects only males, but other types affect both sexes. While some individuals can remain fairly stable for a time, it is a progressive condition in which the muscles become weaker and weaker. The severity of the condition varies from one person to the next and life expectancy also varies a great deal.

Congenital Muscular Dystrophy (CMD)

The symptoms of CMD usually show from birth or within the first six months

- Hypotonia (floppiness)
- Poor head control
- Delayed motor milestones such as crawling and walking
- Tightness in the ankles, hips, knees and elbows
- Sometimes, dislocated hips

There are 3 main types of CMD:

1. Dystrophy – this is solely muscle weakness, but all muscles are affected
2. Muscle weakness plus learning difficulties
3. Muscle weakness, learning difficulties and abnormalities of the eye

The learning difficulties that occur with types 2 and 3 cover the full spectrum, from subtle to severe. The pattern of inheritance is known as 'autosomal recessive': both parents are carriers and have a one in four chance of passing on the condition. It is estimated that one in 50,000 have CMD.

There is no cure but there are ways of alleviating the symptoms through therapy. Physiotherapy and Occupational Therapy (OT) services will be able to assist in school. A child with CMD can remain fairly stable but if the condition rapidly progresses it can lead to respiratory failure.

Some children learn to walk and callipers are often used to help. However, many will be in a wheelchair eventually.

Duchenne's Muscular Dystrophy

This is the most common form of childhood dystrophy and affects only boys. The estimated numbers for this type is one in 3,500 male births. Most children cope well in the early years of school but by the ages of 8 to 11 the majority will be unable to walk.

If there are associated learning difficulties these are often caused by poor communication and language skills from an early age.

As with other types of dystrophies, there is no cure and the severity of the symptoms has to be assessed for each individual.

Becker Muscular Dystrophy

Again, this is a type that affects only males but is milder and progresses far more slowly than Duchenne's MD. This is a fairly rare form and there are often few signs in early childhood other than cramps, being late learning to walk and not being able to run very fast. The symptoms become more evident in the teenage years when a youngster will have difficulty walking fast or climbing stairs.

Again there is no cure at present but with appropriate help those with Becker MD can live to a reasonably old age.

The majority of boys with Becker MD do not have much trouble in school, except that they may not be too successful in PE. A few may have associated learning difficulties but the majority do not.

How can we help?

- Talk to parents – and the child when appropriate.
- Do not assume developments will/will not take place but work with the individual.
- Think about classroom layout, use of stairs, etc. – access is not just about getting into the building.
- Plan ahead – the pace of deterioration can vary greatly.
- Make full use of help and advice from physiotherapists and occupational therapists – they can advise on equipment and adaptations.
- Ensure a programme of regular exercise – especially swimming.
- Use a buddy system.
- Foster positive attitudes in others through PSHE.
- Make after school clubs accessible to prevent isolation at home.
- Make use of computers and, when appropriate, computer aids.
- Incorporate choice – important for self-esteem.
- Facilitate staff counselling – remember strong emotions are roused when working with a child with a progressive condition.

Muscular Dystrophy Group of Great Britain & Northern Ireland
7-11 Prescott Place, London SW4 6BS
Tel: 020 7720 8055
www.muscular-dystrophy.org

Prader-Willi Syndrome (PWS)

Prader-Willi Syndrome (PWS) is a complex genetic disorder resulting from disruption of chromosome 15. It is estimated that one in every 12,000 to 15,000 people has PWS. It occurs in both sexes and all races. Symptoms typically include low muscle tone, short stature, incomplete sexual development, cognitive disabilities, problem behaviors, and a chronic feeling of hunger that can lead to excessive eating and life-threatening obesity.

Children with Prader-Willi syndrome suffer from constant, insatiable hunger. This is caused by disruption of the appetite-controlling part of the brain (hypothalamus). No matter how much they eat, they can never stop thinking about, and craving food. Sometimes it drives them to the point where they will eat soil, paper or almost anything they can put in their mouths. To compound this problem, people with PWS need less food than their peers without the syndrome because their bodies have less muscle and tend to burn fewer calories. (Many children and young adults are now receiving growth hormone therapy to help counteract this.) No appetite suppressant has worked consistently for people with PWS. Most require an extremely low-calorie diet all their lives and access to food must be controlled at all times (many families have to lock the kitchen or the cabinets and refrigerator).

The hypothalamus also controls the body's 'thermostat' and other biological rhythms. PWS may cause a child's temperature to rise very quickly: there are also cases where fever is absent in serious illness or infection. Abnormal sleep patterns may also be a symptom and children can experience daytime sleepiness.

In addition, children with PWS tend to have obsessive/compulsive behaviors such as repetitive thoughts and verbalizations, collecting and hoarding of possessions, picking at skin irritations, and a strong need for routine and predictability. Frustration or changes in plans can easily set off a loss of emotional control, ranging from tears to temper tantrums and physical aggression.

While medication can help some individuals, the essential strategies for minimizing difficult behaviour are careful structuring of the environment and consistent use of positive behaviour management and support.

Providing for a child with PWS usually involves a multidisciplinary approach, with input from a speech and language therapist and occupational therapist as well as medical/dietary experts.

The main characteristics

- Excessive appetite (the drive for food can be mild to very severe)
- Low muscle tone
- Respiratory difficulties (resulting from weak chest muscles)
- Emotional instability and inability to control anger
- Immature physical development
- High pain threshold (this may mask the presence of an injury or infection)
- Under-developed motor skills
- Learning disabilities (sometimes very mild)
- Weak language and communication skills (a result of poor muscle tone [hypotonia] as well as cognitive delays)
- Problems in understanding complex instructions and explanations
- Difficulty in understanding time
- Limited problem-solving capability
- Lack of stamina
- Compulsive tendencies

How can we help?

- Most students with PWS are visual learners: use pictures, videos and hands-on demonstration as much as possible.
- Be aware of problems with balance, coordination and strength, which may affect running, jumping, climbing, skipping, catching and throwing. Drawing, cutting and printing are often frustrating activities. Seek advice from an occupational therapist where appropriate.
- Use clear instructions, broken down into single steps.
- When drowsiness is a problem, change/increase the activity level, e.g. by sending the child on an errand. Build in a 'rest time' during the school day if this is practicable.
- Schedule as much daily exercise as possible.
- Set up a routine and maintain consistency in the classroom environment. Keep change to a minimum. Flag up any changes and allow for discussion.
- Be alert for signs of food-seeking within the classroom and/or the school. Keep food out of sight (pupils' snacks, packed lunches, etc.) and be aware of stimulating the appetite with the smell of food. Avoid using food as rewards.
- Provide supervision during lunchtime.
- When going on visits and field trips, discuss all food-related issues beforehand. Consult with parents/carers.
- Educate and inform all school personnel including secretaries and lunchtime supervisers about any pupil with PWS . Explain to other children in the class/school why a child with PWS behaves as he or she does.
- Teach all children about healthy food choices and nutrition.
- Start off by giving the child less work and add more if you feel he or she will be able to complete in the allotted time. Being unable to finish what has been started often causes anxiety and temper outbursts.

at a glance

- Use 'strategic timing' for activities you know are difficult for the student to stop: e.g. schedule computer time before break, lunch or the end of school so that there is a definite cut-off point.
- Set limits where a child repeats the same question: 'I have answered that question once already, I am going to tell you just one more time.' Ask the child to repeat an answer to you, to demonstrate understanding.
- Stressful situations can lead to emotional 'discontrol'. Help pupils to use words, not behaviour, when communicating emotions. Practise naming and talking about feelings (visual props may prove useful).

- Teach activities that can be used for releasing frustration (ripping paper, going for a walk) in an area that is appropriate for this. Practise those activities before they are needed.
- Use books, stories, role-playing and other creative means to help children understand and express their emotions as well as the emotions of others including interpreting nonverbal communication.

Prader-Willi Syndrome Association (UK)
125a London Road, Derby DE1 2QQ
Tel: 01332 365676
www.pwsa-uk.demon.co.uk

Williams Syndrome

Williams Syndrome is a rare congenital disorder occurring in about one in every 20,000 births. Like Down's syndrome, it is caused by an abnormality in chromosomes and affects several areas of development. It is a non-hereditary syndrome which occurs at random and can affect cognitive and physical development to widely varying degrees.

Reported cases of children with Williams syndrome are increasing in number as more becomes known about the condition and improved identification processes are put in place. It is important that teachers know about the characteristics of Williams Syndrome and understand that these children have particular needs that are different from others with learning difficulties.

The main characteristics

Children with Williams syndrome generally have characteristic facial features, sometimes described as 'elfin', with a small upturned nose, curly hair, full lips, small teeth and especially bright eyes. They usually begin walking later than other toddlers, due to a combination of co-ordination, balance and strength issues. Talking may also be slow to develop, but children with this syndrome tend to be very social and their communication skills often become a strength; this can lead to children being seen as brighter than they actually are. Cognitively, there is a great deal of variation, but all will have some degree of learning difficulty. Some children with Williams Syndrome develop strengths in particular areas such as language, music and interpersonal skills.

The following characteristics are typical of the syndrome but by no means will all be relevant to every child with Williams Syndrome.

- Impaired gross and fine motor skills
- Heightened sensitivity to sounds (hyperacusis)
- Good memory for items learned
- Anxiety about unexpected changes in routine
- Fear of heights and uneven surfaces
- Impaired visuo-spatial skills
- Uneven profile between apparent verbal ability and poorer cognitive skills
- Fixating on certain topics – particularly on things that make them anxious
- A frequent need to urinate
- Difficulty in building and maintaining friendships
- Short concentration span and distractability
- Difficulty in modulating emotions – may become over-anxious, unnecessarily tearful or show extreme excitement when happy
- Problems with numeracy, especially money/time concepts
- Inappropriate behaviour (e.g. talking out of turn, talking to strangers, wandering off, following their own internal 'agenda')

How can we help?

Most children with Williams syndrome require significant support in school and will usually have a statement of special educational needs, detailing their particular requirements. The strategies listed below provide some general guidance.

- Allow for flexibility within the school day/lesson, with frequent breaks between tasks.
- Minimize distractions, both visual and auditory.
- Re-direct when the child is off-task and reward for attentive behaviour.
- Allow some degree of choice of activity wherever possible.
- Teach the child in small groups.
- Help the child to modulate emotions by anticipating frustration and preventing it from escalating.
- Talk through any potentially upsetting situations to prepare the child and rehearse an appropriate response.
- Model appropriate reactions: 'The pot of flowers has tipped over, but never mind, we can mop up the water and put things straight again. No problem.'
- Use stories and role-play to demonstrate appropriate emotional responses.
- Alert the child to predictable noises – fire drill, end of lesson bells, etc.
- Answer questions clearly and check that the child has understood. If the same question is repeated, ignore the repetition and direct the child to another topic.
- Provide appropriate time to discuss a child's favourite topic and use this as a way into different areas of the curriculum where possible.
- Prepare the child for changes to routine and provide with detailed timetables, visual if appropriate.
- Help the child to find his or her way around the school and orientate writing (left to right across the page; letters formed correctly, etc.).
- The sensitive hearing of children with WS can make phonetic approaches to reading and spelling very effective.
- Capitalize on strong memory skills.
- Provide opportunities for children to interact socially in the classroom e.g. paired work, peer tutoring.

Williams Syndrome Foundation
www.williams-syndrome.org.uk
Contact a Family
170 Tottenham Court Road, London W1P OHA
Tel: 0171 383 3555
(Information on rare syndromes affecting children.)

SEN Strategy

Every Child Matters: Change for Children

The Green Paper published in 2003 entitled *Every Child Matters* was the Government's response to Lord Laming's enquiry into the death of Victoria Climbie. When the tragic circumstances surrounding the death of this little girl were made public, there was widespread outrage that public services and support systems had failed to respond effectively. The Green Paper laid the foundations for policies and practices which would protect children and ensure that nothing like this could ever happen again.

Every Child Matters: Change for Children sets out the framework for building services around the needs of children and young people, and the Children Act 2004 provides the legislative foundation that supports the change programme.

The key messages are:

● Child protection cannot be separated from policies to improve children's lives as a whole.
● Agencies must work together to provide services that operate around the needs of the child/young person.

The Government consulted widely, including with children, young people and their families. The five things that they said mattered most to them were:

1. Being healthy.
2. Staying safe.
3. Enjoying and achieving.
4. Making a positive contribution.
5. Economic well-being.

Although there is a *national* drive to improve services, there is a recognition that improved outcomes for children and young people depend on the action taken in *local* change programmes. Voluntary and community organizations are seen as key players as well as public services, as they have significant expertise to offer in developing strategy and planning services.

Alongside the Children Act and *Every Child Matters* sit other key strategies, including:

● *Removing Barriers to Achievement* (see page 65)
● The National Service Framework for Children, Young People and Maternity Services (NSF)
● Choosing Health: making healthy choices easier

Every Child Matters reflects the important relationship between educational achievement and well-being. There is a great deal of evidence to show that educational achievement is the most effective way to improve the outcomes for children living in poverty.

Integrated Services

The Children Act established a *'duty to cooperate'* on all statutory agencies, recognizing that the integration of services would be essential in achieving improved outcomes for all children and young people. The Act also stipulated a shift in services from *intervention* to *prevention* in meeting the needs of the most vulnerable.

Putting the Children Act into action

● Every Authority to appoint a Director for Children's Services and a Lead Member for Children and Young People as well as setting up a Children's Trust.
● Local Safeguarding Children Boards.
● Sure Start and Children's Centres set up to combine health and family support with early education and childcare.
● Extended Schools programme expanded so that eventually every school will be able to offer childcare and facilities from 8am until 6pm (although not necessarily on the school site).
● 14–19 Partnerships ensuring that all young people are supported to realize their potential and develop positively through the teenage years.
● High quality specialist services for children with additional needs, such as those with disabilities.
● Promoting the educational achievements of children who are in public care and building on the messages of the Quality Protects programme.
● Issuing guidance on a set of core skills and knowledge for everyone working with children.
● Providing a Common Assessment Framework (CAF), a national common process for early assessment.
● Improving the practice of sharing information between practitioners in children's services and across local boundaries.
● Facilitating Joint Commissioning and Pooled Budgets.

Planning

Local partners need to balance local and national priorities and publish their conclusions in the Children and Young People's Plan (CYPP). The CYPP is required to cover local authority services for children, young people and their families but in reality the practical involvement of *all* local partners is essential:

● Health services
● Youth justice
● Voluntary organizations
● Community organizations
● Culture, sports and play

www.everychildmatters.gov.uk

Removing Barriers to Achievement

Removing Barriers to Achievement is the Government's strategy for special educational needs, and was launched in February 2004. It sets out the Government's agenda for special educational needs for the following ten years and is intended to complement *Every Child Matters* and the National Service Framework.

The strategy is divided into four chapters that spell out the key messages of:

1. Early intervention
2. Removing barriers to learning
3. Raising expectations and achievement
4. Delivering improvements in partnerships

It is a comprehensive document that can help Local Authorities and schools to improve and develop services for children with special educational needs, working alongside the holistic policies established by *Every Child Matters*.

1. Early intervention

Beginning with access to appropriate and high quality childcare arrangements, this is about services working together to prevent more serious problems developing as a child gets older. The aim is to provide linked services to prevent high numbers of children needing a statement of special educational needs in later years. Some of the strategies suggested are:

- Services arranged around the child and their family as in 'Team Around the Child' (TAC). This is an approach being developed through the Early Support Programmes.
- An extension of the different Early Support Programmes. Eventually it is envisaged that every Authority will adopt at least one of the approaches shown to be of benefit through the Early Support Programme.
- An extension of the Sure Start Programme, including Portage and services for children with Autistic Spectrum Disorders (ASD).
- A co-ordinated approach to children's services through the formation of Children's Trusts.
- Delegation of special education needs (SEN) funding to support early intervention strategies.

2. Removing barriers to learning

The issue here is about embedding inclusive practice and many Authorities are creating Quality Marks that reflect effective inclusion in the way that schools help pupils to learn, achieve and participate in the life of the school.

The role of special schools is changing. Those changes include becoming specialist schools, leading edge schools and developing outreach services. Special schools will share their expertise with clusters of mainstream schools. Special school places will be available for those children and young people with the most severe and complex needs, where their parents wish for one. The Inclusion Development Programme will support partnership projects that help schools meet the needs of pupils with ASD, ESBD, Speech, Language and Communication Difficulties and those with Moderate Learning Difficulties. This is the Government's way of letting schools know that they do not expect children with these needs to be in special schools.

A module on special educational needs in the National College of School Leadership programme will actively promote inclusion. Minimum standards for advisory and support services will be developed.

3. Raising expectations and achievement

This is mainly concerned with ways of developing teachers' skills to meet children's needs, and examines in detail how to build the skills and confidence of the workforce. This aspect is covered in great detail in *Every Child Matters* and a guide to core skills for working with children has been developed. Some of the ways to achieve this are suggested as:

- Better initial training
- A pyramid of skills with an emphasis on Continuing Professional Development (CPD)
- Pupil progress tracked through Personalized Learning
- An improvement in the focus of Transition Reviews

4. Delivering improvements in partnerships

Delivering improvements in partnerships is the area that visibly builds on the recommendations of *Every Child Matters*. Education can no longer work in isolation but must actively work in co-operation with all the major agencies, parents and voluntary organizations to offer the best possible options for children and their families. The government aims to see an end to the 'postcode lottery' where support and services for special educational needs is concerned. In order to do this the following are seen as imperative:

- National SEN advisors to try to ensure consistent practice across the country, especially in areas such as funding.
- A greater emphasis on monitoring, both in terms of value for money and in terms of progress tracking. This will include monitoring of local authorities by Her Majesty's Inspectorate and Ofsted and monitoring of schools by LAs.
- A greater role for SEN Regional Partnerships, with which will come greater accountability, especially concerning the impact of their work.
- Joint services provided by education, social services and health. This will include reform of the workforce and joint training.
- The development of extended schools. The Government wants to see every school eventually offering some form of childcare from 8 am to 6 pm, although it is envisaged that schools will work together in collaboratives and not necessarily provide this on each individual site.
- Parents will be equal partners in all developments and it is important that they have confidence in the services being delivered.

A summary of the strategy is available from:
dfes@prolog.uk.com
or alternatively it can be found at:
www.teachernet.gov.uk/docbank/index.cfm?id=5970

Disability Discrimination

The law

1995 The Disability Discrimination Act (DDA)
Established an accepted definition of disability in law.
Made it unlawful to treat disabled people less favourably for a reason related to their disability.
There were implications for schools and Governors related to parent/public access but not directly related to the pupils at this stage.

1996 The Education Act
The law relating to special educational needs is contained in Part IV and Schedules 26 and 27.

2001 The Special Educational Needs and Disability Act (SENDA)
This Act extended the remit of the DDA 1995 so that it now included schools; therefore it became unlawful to discriminate against a pupil or prospective pupil due to a reason related to their disability.
The Special Educational Needs Tribunal (SENT) also had its remit extended to cover claims of disability discrimination and became known as the Special Educational Needs and Disability Tribunal (SENDIST).

2005 The Disability Discrimination Act
This has extended the definition of disability and the duties of all public services, including the duty to actively promote disability equality.

What is a disability?

The full definition and explanation can be found on the website, www.drc-gb.org, but the core of the definition is '... *a physical or mental impairment, which has a substantial and long-term adverse affect on a person's ability to perform normal day-to-day activities.*'

The 2005 Act extended the definition to include people with HIV, Multiple Sclerosis and some forms of cancer. It also moved away from a reliance on medical definitions of mental impairment.

The definition explains in detail what is meant by substantial and long-term and what constitutes day-to-day activities.

What does it mean for schools?

Since September 2002 it has been unlawful for schools to discriminate against pupils and prospective pupils for a reason related to his/her disability in relation to:
- Admissions
- Education and associated services, including:
  - School trips
  - The curriculum
  - Teaching and learning
  - School sports
  - School meals
  - After school clubs
- Exclusions

What is discrimination?

There are two ways in which a school may be said to discriminate against a pupil for a reason related to their disability:

1. Less favourable treatment that it cannot justify.
2. Failure to take reasonable steps to ensure a pupil is not at a substantial disadvantage compared to other pupils at the school.

Examples

A. A pupil with epilepsy is prevented from attending the outward bounds week with his class because of the potential difficulties.
Reasonable adjustments? The school would have to demonstrate that they had carried out a risk assessment and that there were no adjustments that they could make such as providing a trained support assistant.
It is unlikely that a school could justify this course of action as the steps that could be taken would be considered reasonable.

B. A pupil with ADHD is told that he will have to sit a public examination in the main hall with everyone else despite the fact that special arrangements have been approved.
Reasonable adjustments? The school would have to demonstrate that there was not a single room available anywhere and that no member of staff was available to supervise the pupil.
It is unlikely that the school could possibly justify this as even if space was at a premium, it would be expected that a Deputy or someone with an office could vacate the room for the required time.

C. A deaf pupil lip reads but teachers frequently turn to write on the board and continue speaking.
Reasonable adjustments? It is up to members of staff to adjust their teaching techniques so that they do not put the deaf pupil at a substantial disadvantage. The school would be expected to have arranged some professional training through an appropriate service such as Sensory Services and for the member(s) of staff to have this as a professional target through their performance management review.
If this did not happen the school could find itself at a disability tribunal.

D. A pupil with mobility issues is refused admission to a school because all the specialist mathematics rooms are on the second floor.
Reasonable adjustments? Although schools are not expected to make adjustments to school buildings it would be reasonable to expect for them to arrange for one of the rooms on the ground floor to be made into a mathematics specialist room for the new intake.
Schools must plan long-term changes to physical access through their Accessibility Plan.

Additional duties

Local Authorities and schools must plan to make improvements in terms of accessibility:

● Local Authorities must publish an *Accessibility Strategy*.
● Schools must publish an *Accessibility Plan*.

As with all plans and policies these should be reviewed regularly and must be available to parents. The plans must show how the Local Authority/school is going to:

● Improve access to the curriculum.
● Improve physical access to the school/Authority buildings.
● Improve the range of formats in which information is provided. This may include video, audio tape, large print or Braille.

Local Authorities and schools must show how they will:

● Eliminate unlawful discrimination and harassment against disabled people.
● Promote equality of opportunity for disabled people.
● Promote positive attitudes to disabled people.
● Encourage disabled people to participate fully in public life.

An annual report must show how the Authority/school is making progress to promote disability equality and address disability discrimination.

What does this mean for schools?

Someone needs to take responsibility for reviewing and revising the Accessibility Plan and have responsibility for promoting disability equality, although it is imperative that *everyone* is involved in the process and that it reflects a whole school ethos.

The Special Educational Needs Co-ordinator (SENCO) must ensure that all staff are trained in and are aware of disability issues and how they may affect the pupils with whom they work. This would include knowledge of specific conditions such as dyslexia, autistic spectrum disorders, ADHD, etc.

'All staff' must include everyone a pupil is likely to come into contact with, including administration staff, lunchtime supervisors and cleaning staff. Remember, many incidents happen in the dinner queue or in the playground!

The school should have a rolling professional development programme to ensure disability issues are frequently revisited.

All school policies should reflect disability equality and awareness.

Council for Disabled Children (CDC)
National Children's Bureau,
8 Wakeley Street,
London EC1V 7EQ
Tel: 020 7843 6058
www.ncb.org.uk/cdc

The Code of Practice for Special Educational Needs

The Code of Practice for Special Educational Needs (DfES, 2001) states that children with special educational needs should:

- have their needs met, normally in a mainstream school or setting.
- be offered full access to a broad, balanced and relevant education (including an appropriate curriculum for the Foundation Stage, and the National Curriculum).

The Code of Practice also states that parents have a vital role to play in supporting their child's education, and the views of the child should be sought and taken into account

(See Code of Practice at 4:27 for early years, 5:50 for primary and 6:58 for secondary guidance).

Most children will be able to access the curriculum and achieve success in their work if the teacher differentiates appropriately. There are various ways of matching the task to the abilities of a child. These involve different approaches concerning:

- time allowed for completion of tasks and the pace of a lesson/ activity
- level of support provided and resources used
- type of task set for the pupil
- expected outcomes

Where children do not make satisfactory progress, in spite of good teaching and appropriate differentiation, the Code sets out a continuum of intervention within three broad levels:

- **School Action/Early Years Action**: a child is identified as needing extra support and this is provided within the school.
- **School Action Plus/Early Years Action Plus**: after a period of extra support, the school seeks advice/support from external agencies such as the Learning Support Service, Speech and Language Therapist or Behaviour Support Team. An Individual Education Plan (IEP) is formulated.
- In a minority of cases, pupils are assessed by a multi-disciplinary team on behalf of the local education authority, whose officers then decide whether or not to issue a **statement of SEN**. This is a legally binding document which details the child's needs and specifies the resources to be provided. It is reviewed at least once a year at an annual review meeting.

Annual Review Meeting

This meeting should involve the pupil, parents/carers, classteacher/ form tutor, the Special Educational Needs Coordinator (SENCO), and any teaching assistants working with the child. Invitations may also be sent out to therapists working with the pupil, the educational psychologist, Local Authority officers, and sometimes the pupil's paediatrician. When these professionals are unable to attend the meeting, they may send written reports.

In addition to reviewing the statement, those at the annual review meeting will discuss the pupil's current IEP, make suggestions for new or amended targets and identify the areas of greatest need for the pupil over the following twelve months.

Once the long-term targets are agreed at the annual review, the SENCO and classteacher/form tutor can then:

- set new short-term targets
- identify strategies to be used: resources, context for support (in-class, small group, one to one, etc.)
- decide on how much and how often support is to be given
- identify staff members who will support the pupil in achieving the targets (peer support, teaching assistants, learning support service teachers, etc.)
- plan ways in which parents can support the pupil to achieve the targets
- arrange monitoring procedures

Individual Education Plans

An IEP describes actions to be taken, over and above the day-to-day differentiation in the class, in order to enable a child to make progress. (Group Education Plans (GEPs) are drawn up where several children in the class have common targets for which common strategies are appropriate.) The best IEPs are planning, teaching and reviewing tools which include two or three SMART targets (Specific, Measurable, Achievable, Relevant and Timed), usually relating to the key areas of communication, literacy, mathematics, physical skills, and behaviour and social skills.

Targets should be clear to all concerned, in jargon-free language. The pupil should be able to tell parents, 'Today I learned how to. . .', or 'I learned that. . .'. In this way, pupils and their parents will be involved in the process and can work together toward achieving the

---

Emma, who has Down's Syndrome, has difficulty remembering what books and equipment to take to her mainstream secondary school each day. She frequently gets into trouble for not having everything she needs – especially for PE and food technology. When Emma met with her form tutor to discuss IEP targets, this issue of personal organization was seen as important by both parties. They agreed that one of Emma's targets would be, 'Emma will arrive at lessons with the books and equipment she needs.' Strategies could then be employed to support Emma in achieving her goal. A photographic cue card could be made for her, showing and listing the resources needed for each day. A copy of this card could be kept at home, and her parents could help to pack Emma's school bag each evening – or at least check that everything was there. Achieving this target would have a significant impact on learning, self-esteem, independence and the way in which Emma is perceived by teachers. It is a not a subject-specific target, but one which all teachers should be aware of and able to support, recording after each lesson whether or not Emma has met her target and giving positive reinforcement whenever possible.

(This example is adapted from Briggs, S. (2004) *Inclusion and How to Do It: Meeting SEN in Secondary Classrooms*. London: David Fulton Publishers.)

targets (see example below). There should be details of strategies for meeting these targets, clear success criteria and a review date. An IEP or GEP should therefore always state what is to be done, when it will happen and be reviewed and who will be involved. This should be written in jargon-free language, with any 'technical' terms fully explained.

IEPs should be working documents, distributed to all staff working with the student and constantly at hand. Teachers, teaching assistants, parents and pupils themselves should be involved in the monitoring and review of IEPs.

Individual behaviour plans

Where pupils have behaviour problems in addition to learning difficulties, they may have an Individual Behaviour Plan as well as an IEP. This can result in the pupil having more targets than he or she can manage, and little will be achieved. Keeping a balance of curricular and behaviour targets within the IEP gives a greater chance that the target-setting will be successful, and behaviour difficulties often improve dramatically when the child begins to achieve success with his or her work.

P-scales

P-scales help teachers to set appropriate and achievable targets for pupils with learning difficulties and report on progress made, even if progress is made in very small steps. They provide a framework of common performance measures for benchmark information, and for the calculation of value-added improvement for pupils working at these levels. The P-scales offer ready-made objectives for using in IEPs and help teachers to differentiate work for pupils within a wide range of ability. (see www.qca.org.uk)

Differentiation strategies

- Check the readability of texts used in the classroom and support weak readers
- Provide word banks and spell checkers
- Enlarge print and/or use coloured paper or overlays
- Simplify text and worksheets, using clear instructions
- Adapt equipment and/or obtain special equipment (sensory support services and physiotherapy units may help with this)
- Use visual props and/or symbols to support understanding
- Provide writing frames to support recording
- Offer alternative means of recording (e.g. audio tapes, voice recognition software, diagrammatic/mind map recording, digital photographs of completed work and investigations in progress)
- Use touch screens, switches and large-format keyboards
- Use software such as Clicker (Crick Software) to support writing
- Adapt tasks or provide alternative activities – breaking down new learning into small chunks
- Use a multi-sensory approach (sometimes known as VAK – visual, auditory, kinaesthetic)
- Provide targeted support from adults or peers
- Allow extra time for completion of tasks and/or provide opportunities for preparation time, perhaps with the help of a teaching assistant

Appendices

INDIVIDUAL EDUCATION PLAN

Name:	Start date:	Area of concern:
Year:	Review date:	Strengths:
Stage:	IEP no.:	Teacher/Support:

| Success criteria: | Strategies for use in class: | Role of Parent(s)/Carer(s): |
| | | |

Targets:	Resources:	Agreed by:
		SENCO:
		Parent(s)/Carer(s):
		Pupil:
		Date:

Glossary

AAC	Augmented and Alternative Communication		**LCSB**	Local Children's Safeguarding Board
ADD	Attention Deficit Disorder		**LP**	Lead Professional
ADHD	Attention Deficit Hyperactivity Disorder		**LSA**	Learning Support Assistant
			LSS	Learning Support Service
AS	Asperger's Syndrome		**LSU**	Learning Support Unit
ASD	Autistic Spectrum Disorder		**LVA**	Low Vision Aids
BAC	Behaviour and Attendance Consultant		**MAST**	Multi-agency Support Team
			MD	Muscular Dystrophy
BATOD	British Association of Teachers of the Deaf		**Mentor**	An assistant whose brief is motivation and behaviour as opposed to learning support in the classroom
BESD	Behavioural, Emotional and/or Social Difficulties			
BEST	Behaviour and Education Support Team		**MLD**	Moderate Learning Difficulties
			Monocular vision	Sight in one eye only
BIP	Behaviour Improvement Programme			
CAF	Common Assessment Framework		**Myopia**	Shortsightedness
CAMHS	Child and Adolescent Mental Health Services		**NAS**	National Autistic Society
			Nystagmus	Involuntary movement of the eye
CP	Cerebral Palsy		**OT**	Occupational Therapist
CSA	Children's Services Authority		**PEP**	Personal Education Plan (for LAC)
CT	Children's Trust			
CYPP	Children and Young People's Plan		**PMLD**	Profound and Multiple Learning Difficulties
CYPSP	Children and Young People's Strategic Partnership			
			PRS	Pupil Referral Service
DDA	Disability Discrimination Act		**PRU**	Pupil Referral Unit
EBSD	Emotional, Behavioural and Social Difficulties		**QTVI**	Qualified Teacher of Visual Impairment
ECM	Every Child Matters		**RBA**	Removing Barriers to Achievement
ECM: CFC	Every Child Matters: Change for Children			
			SALT/SLT	Speech and Language Therapist
EP	Educational Psychologist		**SEF**	Self Evaluation Form
ESP	Early Support Programme		**SENCO**	Special Educational Needs Coordinator
ESW	Education Social Worker			
EWO	Education Welfare Officer		**SENDA**	Special Educational Needs Disability Act
EYDCP	Early Years Development and Childcare Partnership		**SENDIST**	Special Educational Needs and Disability Tribunal
GLD	Global Learning Difficulties			
HI	Hearing Impairment		**SENSS**	Special Educational Needs Support Service
IBP	Individual Behaviour Plan			
ICT	Information and Communication Technology		**SLD**	Severe Learning Difficulties
			SpLD	Specific Learning Difficulties (e.g. Dyslexia)
IEP	Individual Education Plan			
ISA	Information Sharing Arrangements		**SSA**	Special Support Assistant
			TA	Teaching Assistant
ISI	Information Sharing Index		**TAC**	Team Around the Child
JAR	Joint Area Review		**VI**	Visual Impairment
LAC	Looked After Children		**YOT**	Youth Offending Team

Directory

Advisory Unit Computers in Education (AUCE)

The Advisory Unit is an independent organization offering ICT services and educational software to schools. Their objective is to provide a comprehensive service to help teachers use computers effectively.
Advisory Unit Computers in Education (AUCE)
126 Great North Road
Hatfield
Hertfordshire AL9 5JZ
Tel: 01707 266 714
www.advisory-unit.org.uk

AFASIC

For children and young people with speech and language impairments and their families.
Afasic
2nd Floor
50-52 Great Sutton St
London EC1V ODJ
Tel: (administration) 020 7490 9411
Helpline: 0845 355 5577 (local call rate)
Fax: 020 7251 2834
Email: info@afasic.org.uk
www.afasic.org.uk

ACE Centre (Aiding Communication in Education)

The Oxford ACE Centre provides a focus for the use of technology in meeting the needs of young people with physical and communication difficulties.
ACE Centre
92 Windmill Road
Headington
Oxford OX3 7DR
Tel: 01865 759 800
Fax: 01865 759810
Email: info@ace-centre.org.uk
www.ace-centre.org.uk

ADDNET UK

ADDNet is the UK's national website for Attention Deficit (Hyperactivity) Disorder. The purpose of the website is to be a common point of reference for information and intelligent debate on AD/HD in the UK.
ADDNET
Tel: 020 8269 1400
Email: addnet@web-v.co.uk
www.btinternet.com/~black.ice/addnet

Advisory Centre for Education (ACE)

An independent national advice centre for parents.
ACE
1C Aberdeen Studios
22 Highbury Grove
London N5 2DQ
Tel (administration): 020 7354 8318
Freephone: 0808 800 5793
Fax: 020 7354 9069
www.ace-ed.org.uk
Email: ace-ed@easynet.co.uk
www.ace-centre.org.uk
Information on exclusions: 0808 8000 327
Exclusion information line: 020 7704 9822

Alliance for Inclusive Education

The organization is composed of disabled people, their parents and campaigners. The alliance's aim is to end compulsory segregation in the education system.
ALLFIE
Unit 2, 70 South Lambeth Road
London SW8 1RL
Tel: 020 7735 5277
Fax: 020 7735 3828
www.allfie.org.uk

Asthma and Allergy Information and Research (AAIR)

The objectives of AAIR and those of its parent organization are to further education and research in asthma and allergic diseases, and it provides support for patients in certain areas.
AAIR
12 Vernon Street
Derby DE1 1FT
Tel: 0116 270 7557 or 0116 270 9338
Email: aair@globalnet.co.uk
www.users.globalnet.co.uk/~aair

Autism Independent UK

The Society exists to increase awareness of autism, together with well-established and newly-developed approaches in the diagnosis, assessment, education and treatment.
AI UK
199-205 Blandford Avenue
Kettering
Northants NN16 9AT
Tel: 01536 523274
Email: autism@autismuk.com
www.autismuk.com

British Dyslexia Institute

The Dyslexia Institute (DI) is an educational charity, founded in 1972, for the assessment and teaching of people with dyslexia and for the training of teachers. For a list of centres around the country please visit:
Email: info@dyslexia-inst.org.uk
www.dyslexia-inst.org.uk/contacts.htm

BILD (British Institute of Learning Disabilities)

BILD provide services that promote good practice in the provision and planning of the health and social care services for people with learning disabilities.
BILD
Campion House, Green Street
Kidderminster
Worcestershire DY10 1SL
Tel: 01562 723 010
Fax: 01562 723 029
Email:bild@bild.org.co.uk
www.bild.org.uk

British Epilepsy Association

New Anstey House
Gate Way Drive
Yeadon, Leeds LS19 7XY
Tel: 0113 210 8800
Freephone: 0808 800 5050
Fax: 0113 391 0300
Email: helpline@epilepsy.org.uk
www.epilepsy.org.uk

British Stammering Association (BSA)

BSA's mission is to initiate and support research into stammering, to identify and promote effective therapies, offer support to those whose lives are affected by stammering and help teachers to be more responsive to the needs of stammering pupils.
BSA
15 Old Ford Road
London E2 9PJ
Tel: 020 8983 1003
Helpline: 0845 603 2001
Fax: 020 8983 3591
Email: mail@stammering.org
www.stammering.org/homepage.html

CAF (Contact a Family)

Every day over 60 children in the UK are born or diagnosed with a serious disability and the vast majority of them are cared for at home. Contact a Family is the only UK charity providing support and advice to parents whatever the medical condition of their child.
CAF
209-211 City Road
London EC1V 1JN
Tel: 020 7608 700
Helpline: 0808 808 3555
Fax: 020 7608 701
Email: info@cafamily.org.uk

Contact a Family Wales

Contact a Family Cymru
Room 153 S
1st Floor
The Exchange Building
Mount Stuart Square
Cardiff CF10 5EB
Tel: 029 2049 8001
www.cafamily.org.uk/wales

Centre for Studies on Inclusive Education (CSIE)

CSIE is a British independent educational charity, a national centre funded mainly by donations. It gives information and advice about inclusive education and related issues.
http://inclusion.uwe.ac.uk/csie/csiehome.htm

The Children's Society

The Children's Society
Edward Rudolf House
Margery Street
London WC1X 0JL
Tel: 020 7841 4400
Fax: 020 7837 0211
www.the-childrens-society.org.uk

Children with Diabetes

The organization's website aims to develop contact for parents and children who live with diabetes.
www.childrenwithdiabetes.co.uk

Conductive Education

Conductive Education is a form of special education and rehabilitation for children and adults with motor disorders.
Foundation for Conductive Education
Cannon Hill House
Russell Road
Moseley
Birmingham B13 8RD
Tel: 0121 449 1569
Fax: 0121 449 1611
Email: foundation@conductive-education.org.uk
www.conductive-education.org.uk

Council for Disabled Children

The Council for Disabled Children promotes collaborative work between different organizations providing services and support for children and young people with disabilities and special educational needs.
www.ncb.org.uk/cdc

Diabetes UK

The charity works for people with diabetes, funding research, campaigning and helping people live with the condition.
Diabetes UK
10 Parkway
London NW1 7AA
Tel: 020 7742 41000
Email: info@diabetes.org.uk
www.diabetes.org.uk/home.htm

Disability Rights Commission

The commission gives advice and information to disabled people, employers and service providers and supports disabled people in getting their rights under the DDA.
Disability Rights Commission
FREEPOST
MID 02164
Stratford upon Avon CV37 9BR
Tel: 08457 622 633
Textphone: 08457 622 644
www.drc-gb.org

Down's Syndrome Association

The Association exists to support parents and carers of people with Down's Syndrome and improve the lives of people with the condition.
The Down's Syndrome Association
Langdon Down Centre,
2a Langdon Park,
Teddington TW11 9PS
Tel: 020 8682 4001
Fax: 020 8682 4012
Email: info@downs-syndrome.org.uk
www.downsed.org

Dyslexia Institute (DI)

Head Office
Park house, Wick road,
Egham, Surrey
Tel: 01784 222 300
Fax: 01784 222 333
www.dyslexia-inst.org.uk

Dyspraxia Trust

The Dyspraxia Trust exists to support individuals and families affected by developmental dyspraxia and to increase understanding about it.
The Dyspraxia Foundation
8 West Alley Hitchin
Herts SG5 1EG
Tel: 01462 454 986
Fax: 01462 455 052
Email: dyspraxiafoundation@hotmail.com
www.emmbrook.demon.co.uk/dysprax/homepage.htm

Education Otherwise

This is a self-help organization for parents educating their children at home.
Education Otherwise
PO Box 7420
London N9 9SG
Tel: 0870 7300074
www.education-otherwise.org

Foundation for People with Learning Disabilities

The Foundation for People with Learning Disabilities works to improve the lives of people with learning disabilities through:

● Funding innovative research and service development projects
● Listening to people with learning disabilities and involving them in its work
● Seeking to influence policy.

The Foundation for People with Learning Disabilities
9th Floor, Sea Containers House
20 Upper Ground
London SEI 9QB
Tel: 020 7802 31100
Email: fpld@fpld.org.uk
www.learningdisabilities.org.uk

Home Education Advisory Service (HEAS)

HEAS offers information for home educators including advice about educational materials, resources, GCSE examinations, special educational needs, information technology, legal matters and curriculum design.
HEAS
PO Box 98
Welwyn Garden City
Hertfordshire AL8 6AN
Tel: 01707 3718854
www.heas.org.uk

I CAN

I CAN is the national educational charity for children with speech and language difficulties.
I CAN
4 Dyer's Buildings
Holborn
London EC1N 2QP
Tel: 0870 225 4072
Fax: 0870 010 4067
Email: http://www.ican.org.uk/emailus/emailican.html
www.ican.org.uk

Independent Panel for Special Education Advice (IPSEA)

IPSEA provides free independent advice on appealing to the Special Educational Needs Tribunal, including representation when needed and free second professional opinions.
IPSEA
6 Carlow Mews
Woodbridge
Suffolk IP12 1DH
Tel: 0800 018 4016
Helpline: 0800 0184016 or 01394 382814
Tribunal appeals only: 01394 384711
General enquiries: 01394 380518
www.ipsea.org.uk

MENCAP

Mencap works with people with a learning disability to fight discrimination. It campaigns to ensure that their rights are recognized and that they are respected as individuals.
Mencap
123 Golden Lane
London EC1Y 0RT
Tel: 020 7454 0454
Fax: 020 7696 5540
www.mencap.org.uk

NAGC (National Association for Gifted Children)

The Association recognizes that the needs of gifted children are best met when parents, students, education professionals, schools and colleges are able to share a common forum and gain wider understanding of home/school issues.
National Association for Gifted Children
Suite 14, Challenge House
Sherwood Drive
Bletchley
Buckinghamshire MK3 6DP
Tel: 0845 450 0221
Fax: 0870 770 3219
Email: amazingchildren@nagcbritain.org.uk
www.nagcbritain.org.uk

National Association for Special Educational Needs (NASEN)

NASEN aims to promote the education, training, advancement and development of all those with special educational needs.
NASEN House
4/5 Amber Business Village
Amber Close
Amington
Tamworth B77 4RP
Tel: 01827 311 500
Fax: 01827 313 005
Email: welcome@nasen.org.uk
www.nasen.org.uk

National Autistic Society (NAS)

The charity's objective is to provide education, treatment, welfare and care to people with autism and related conditions.
NAS
393 City Road
London EC1V 1NG
Tel: 020 7833 2299
Fax: 020 7833 9666
Email: nas@nas.org.uk

National Bureau for Students with Disabilities (SKILL)

Skill is a national charity promoting opportunities for young people and adults with any kind of disability in post-16 education, training and employment across the UK.
Skill
Chapter House
18-20 Crucifix Lane
London SE1 3JW
Tel: 020 7450 0620
www.skill.org.uk

National Children's Bureau (NCB)

The NCB is a registered charity which promotes the interests and well-being of all children and young people across every aspect of their lives.
National Children's Bureau
8 Wakley Street
London EC1V 7QE
Tel: 020 7843 6000
Fax: 020 7278 9512
www.ncb.org.uk

The National Centre for Young People with Epilepsy

NCYPE is a national charity providing specialist services for children and young people with complex epilepsy.
The National Centre for Young People with Epilepsy
St Piers Lane
Lingfield
Surrey RH7 6PW
Tel: 01342 832243
Fax: 01342 834639
Email: info@ncype.org.uk
www.ncype.org.uk

National Deaf Children's Society

The charity is dedicated to supporting all deaf children, young deaf people and their families in overcoming the challenges of childhood deafness.
The National Deaf Children's Society
15 Dufferin Street
London EC1Y 8UR
Tel: 020 7490 8656
Info & Helpline: 0808 800 8880(v/t)
Fax: 020 7251 5020
Email: fundraising@ndcs.org.uk
www.ndcs.org.uk

OASIS (Office for Advice, Assistance Support and Information on Special needs)

Helpline: 09068 633201
Fax: 01590 622687

Rathbone Society

Rathbone is a national charity and voluntary organization which believes that progess is possible for all people.
Rathbone
4th Floor
Churchgate House
56 Oxford Street
Manchester M1 6EU
Tel: 0161 236 5358
Fax: 0161 238 6356

Royal Association for Disability and Rehabilitation (RADAR)

RADAR is an organization of disabled people campaigning for social inclusion, developing best practice and disseminating information.
RADAR
12 City Forum
250 City Road
London EC1V 8AF
Tel: 020 7250 3222
www.radar.org.uk

Royal National Institute for the Blind (RNIB)

RNIB's task is to challenge blindness. They challenge the disabling effects of sight loss by providing information and practical services to help people get on with their own lives.
Tel: 0845 766 9999 (UK Helpline callers only)
Tel: 0207 388 1266 (switchboard/overseas callers)
Fax: 0207 388 2034
Email: helpline@rnib.org.uk

Royal National Institute for the Deaf (RNID)

RNID is the largest charity representing the 8.7 million deaf and hard of hearing people in the UK.
RNID
19-23 Featherstone Street
London EC1Y 8SL
Tel: 0808 808 0123
Fax: 020 7296 8199
Email: informationline@rnid.org.uk
Regional Offices: www.rnib.org.uk/rnid/address.htm

SCOPE

Scope is the national disability organization whose focus is people with cerebral palsy. Their aim is that disabled people achieve equality, in a society in which they are as valued and have the same human and civil rights as everyone else.
Helpline: 0808 800 3333
Email: cphelpline@scope.org.uk
www.scope.org.uk

Scottish Dyslexia Association (SDA)

The SDA provides information and advice to parents, adults, teachers, professional and non-professional people.
SDA
Unit 3, Stirling Business Centre
Wellgreen
Stirling FK8 2DZ
Tel: 01786 446650
Fax: 01786 471235
Helpline: 08448 00 84 84
Email: dyslexia.scotland@dial.pipex.com
www.dyslexia-scotland.org

Scottish Society for Autism (SSA)

The SSA seeks to ensure the provision of the best education, care, support and opportunities for people of all ages with autism in Scotland.
SSA
Alloa Business Centre
The Whins
Alloa FK10 3SA
Tel: 01259 720044
Fax: 01259 720051
www.autism-in-scotland.org.uk

Special Educational Needs and Disability Tribunal (SENDIST)

Parents whose children have special educational needs can appeal to against decisions made by Local Authorities in England and Wales about their children's education. The tribunal is independent of both central and local government.
SENDIST
Procession House
55 Ludgate Hill
London EC4M 7JW
Disability helpline: 0870 606 5750
www.sendist.gov.uk